Math Expressions

Volume 2

Developed by
The Children's Math Worlds Research Project

PROJECT DIRECTOR AND AUTHOR
Dr. Karen C. Fuson

This material is based upon work supported by the
National Science Foundation
under Grant Numbers
ESI-9816320, REC-9806020, and RED-935373.

Any opinions, findings, and conclusions, or recommendations expressed in this material
are those of the author and do not necessarily reflect the views of the National Science Foundation.

 HOUGHTON MIFFLIN HARCOURT

Teacher Reviewers

Kindergarten
Patricia Stroh Sugiyama
Wilmette, Illinois

Barbara Wahle
Evanston, Illinois

Grade 1
Sandra Budson
Newton, Massachusetts

Janet Pecci
Chicago, Illinois

Megan Rees
Chicago, Illinois

Grade 2
Molly Dunn
Danvers, Massachusetts

Agnes Lesnick
Hillside, Illinois

Rita Soto
Chicago, Illinois

Grade 3
Jane Curran
Honesdale, Pennsylvania

Sandra Tucker
Chicago, Illinois

Grade 4
Sara Stoneberg Llibre
Chicago, Illinois

Sheri Roedel
Chicago, Illinois

Grade 5
Todd Atler
Chicago, Illinois

Leah Barry
Norfolk, Massachusetts

Special Thanks

Special thanks to the many teachers, students, parents, principals, writers, researchers, and work-study students who participated in the Children's Math Worlds Research Project over the years.

Credits

(t) © David Hancock/Alamy, (b) Kitch Bain/Alamy.

Illustrative art: Ginna Magee and Burgandy Beam/Wilkinson Studio; Geoff Smith, Tim Johnson
Technical art: Anthology, Inc.

ISBN: 978-0-547-06068-2

14 15 1421 17 16 15 14 13
4500417751

VOLUME 2 CONTENTS

* This lesson consists only of activities from the Teacher Edition.

* This lesson consists only of activities from the Teacher Edition.

Extension Lessons

Glossary

* This lesson consists only of activities from the Teacher Edition.

Class Activity

Name _____

1. **Compare** Mara's crayons with Todd's.
   Complete the sentences below.
   Ring the word **more** or **fewer**.

Mara

Todd

Mara has ⬜ **more** **fewer** apples than Todd.

Todd has ⬜ **more** **fewer** apples than Mara.

---

2. Each ant gets 1 crumb.
   How many more crumbs are needed? ⬜

3. Draw circles on the graph.

Crumbs	🍞 🍞 🍞 🍞
Ants	🐜 🐜 🐜 🐜 🐜 🐜 🐜 🐜 🐜 🐜

---

4. Each bee gets 1 flower. How many extra flowers are there? ⬜

5. Ring the extra flowers.

Flowers	🌹 🌹 🌹 🌹 🌹 🌹 🌹 🌹 🌹
Bees	🐝 🐝 🐝 🐝

6. **On the Back** Lee has 4 blocks. Ben has 2 more blocks than Lee.
   Draw Lee's and Ben's blocks.

Simple Comparisons and Graphs

Dear Family:

In the current math unit, your child is learning to compare data. To begin, children read and construct picture graphs that contain only two rows of symbols, and they learn to make comparative statements. For the graph below, they make statements such as *Paul has 3 more apples than Sara,* and *Sara has 3 fewer apples than Paul.*

Children learn that they can make the quantities on the graph equal if they add to one group or subtract from the other. They use equations to show their method.

$$5 + 3 = 8 \qquad 8 - 3 = 5$$

Then children begin working with picture graphs that contain three or four rows of symbols. When children are asked to compare only two quantities out of three or four, they must select necessary information and disregard information that is unnecessary. Finally, children record and compare quantities using tables.

As your child does the homework, ask him or her to tell you about the picture graphs and tables.

Sincerely,
Your child's teacher

Carta a la familia

Estimada familia:

En esta unidad de matemáticas, su niño está aprendiendo a comparar datos. Para empezar, los niños leen y hacen gráficas ilustradas que tienen dos filas de símbolos y aprenden a formular enunciados comparativos. Para la gráfica de abajo, hacen enunciados como *Pablo tiene 3 manzanas más que Sara y Sara tiene 3 manzanas menos que Pablo.*

Los niños aprenden que pueden hacer que las cantidades de la gráfica sean iguales si suman a un grupo o restan al otro. Usan ecuaciones para mostrar su método.

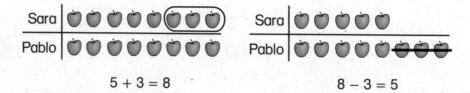

$$5 + 3 = 8 \qquad\qquad 8 - 3 = 5$$

Luego, los niños trabajan con gráficas ilustradas que tienen tres o cuatro filas de símbolos. Cuando se les pide que comparen solamente dos cantidades de tres o cuatro, tienen que seleccionar la información necesaria y descartar la información que no lo es. Por último, los niños anotan y comparan las cantidades utilizando tablas.

A medida que su niño hace la tarea, pídale que le hable sobre las gráficas ilustradas y las tablas.

Atentamente,
El maestro de su niño

Simple Comparisons and Graphs

Class Activity

Name _____

Vocabulary
picture graph
more
fewer

1. Make a **picture graph** about the shapes.

Circles						
Triangles						

2. Complete the sentences. Ring the word **more** or **fewer**.

There are [ ] **more** **fewer** circles than triangles.

There are [ ] **more** **fewer** triangles than circles.

3. Make a picture graph about the food.

Apples						
Carrots						

4. Complete the sentences. Ring the word **more** or **fewer**.

There are [ ] **more** **fewer** apples than carrots.

There are [ ] **more** **fewer** carrots than apples.

5. **On the Back** Mia has 6 blocks. Jamal has 2 fewer blocks. Draw Mia's and Jamal's blocks.

Construct Picture Graphs

Extra Practice

Vocabulary

graph
more
fewer

1. Count the cats and dogs.
Draw circles on the **graph** to show the number of dogs and cats.

Dogs								
Cats								

2. Complete the sentences. Ring the word **more** or **fewer**.

There are [　] **more fewer** cats than dogs.

There are [　] **more fewer** dogs than cats.

3. **On the Back** Draw 8 triangles in a row. Draw 5 circles in a row. Write the word **more** next to the group that has more.

Quick Graphs and Comparisons **209**

Quick Graphs and Comparisons

Name

Class Activity

Eggs Laid This Month

Clucker	⬭ ⬭ ⬭ ⬭
Vanilla	⬭ ⬭ ⬭ ⬭ ⬭ ⬭ ⬭ ⬭ ⬭
Daisy	⬭ ⬭ ⬭ ⬭ ⬭ ⬭ ⬭

Animals in the Pond

Frogs	🐸 🐸 🐸 🐸 🐸 🐸
Fish	🐟 🐟 🐟 🐟 🐟 🐟 🐟
Ducks	🦆 🦆 🦆 🦆
Turtles	🐢 🐢 🐢 🐢 🐢 🐢

Hot Dogs Sold at the Fair

Eric	🌭 🌭 🌭 🌭 🌭 🌭 🌭 🌭
Miranda	🌭 🌭 🌭 🌭 🌭 🌭
Adam	🌭 🌭 🌭 🌭 🌭

Extra Practice

Name _____

1. Draw circles to show how many of each color.

Colors in the Bag									
Red									
Yellow									
Blue									

Use the graph to answer the questions below.

2. How many red cubes are in the bag? _____

3. How many yellow cubes are in the bag? _____

4. How many blue cubes are in the bag? _____

5. Are there **more** red cubes than yellow cubes? _____

6. Are there **fewer** red cubes than blue cubes? _____

7. There are the **most** of which color? _____

8. There are the **fewest** of which color? _____

Graphs with Multiple Rows

Name _____

Class Activity

1. Work together in a group. Use the empty
   graph. Show the number of letters
   in your first names.

Number of Letters in Our Names								
Kristy	○	○	○	○	○	○		
Jeff	○	○	○	○				
Samantha	○	○	○	○	○	○	○	○
Rolando	○	○	○	○	○	○	○	

Number of Letters in Our Names									

2. Explain how the graph makes it easier to
   compare the number of letters in each name.

_____

- -

_____

Name _____

Going Further

Vocabulary

compare
is less than (<)
is greater than (>)

You can use symbols when you **compare** numbers.

A	l	i	c	e

J	o	n	a	t	h	a	n

5 letters   8 letters

5 **is less than** 8

5 < 8

P	a	t	r	i	c	k

A	n	g	e	l	a

7 letters   6 letters

7 **is greater than** 6

7 > 6

Use > or < to compare the numbers.

1. 4 ◯ 9   2. 12 ◯ 8   3. 16 ◯ 6

4. 5 ◯ 2   5. 15 ◯ 11   6. 14 ◯ 15

7. 9 ◯ 10   8. 13 ◯ 10   9. 12 ◯ 21

10. Explain how you remember what each symbol means.

_____

- - - - - - - - - - - - - - - - - -

Student-Generated Graphs

6–7 Class Activity

Name ____________________

Vocabulary
table
graph

1. Make a **table** from the class favorite season **graph**.

Favorite Season Table

Season	Number
Fall	
Winter	
Spring	
Summer	

2. Make a table from the picture graph below.

Picture Graph

Table

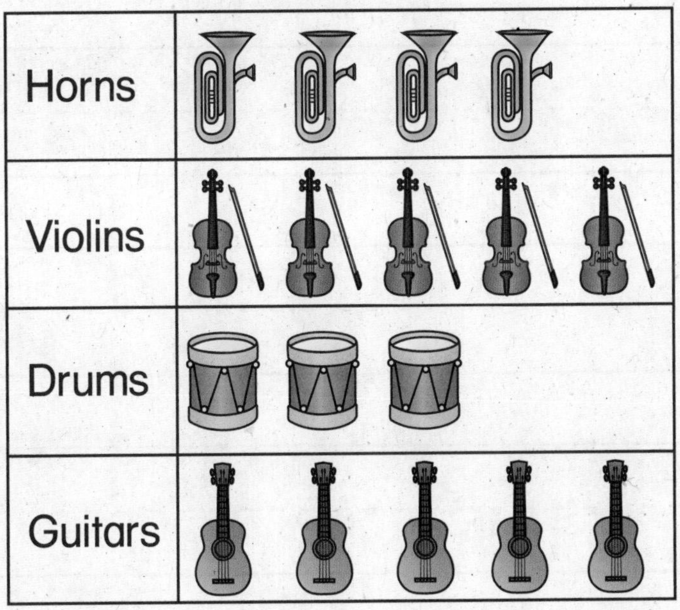

Instruments	Number

3. On the Back Write and answer a question using the favorite season table. Then write and answer a question using the musical instruments table.

Name _____

(ruled writing lines)

Class Activity

Name _____

Solve the story problems.
Use the pictures to help you.

1. Emily made 6 pancakes. Luis made 4 **more** than Emily. How many pancakes did Luis make?

6 _____
label

2. Ana wrapped 7 gifts. Dan wrapped 5 gifts. How many **fewer** gifts did Dan wrap than Ana?

7 fewer _____
label

3. Tessa has 10 CDs. Noah has 3 fewer than Tessa. How many CDs does Noah have?

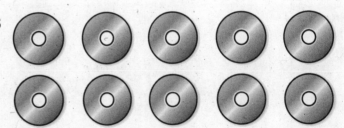

10 _____
label

4. **On the Back** Draw 9 squares. Draw 3 fewer circles.

Story Problems with Comparisons

Class Activity

Name _____

Solve the story problems.
Use drawings and numbers.

1. Cory's cat has 8 kittens.
Eva's cat has 3 kittens.
How many more kittens does
Cory's cat have than Eva's?

   more _____
   label

2. There were 16 bicycles here
yesterday. There are 7 **fewer**
bicycles here today. How many
bicycles are here today?

   _____
   label

3. Ms. Perez has 15 horses.
Mr. Drew has 9 horses.
How many **more** horses does
Ms. Perez have than Mr. Drew?

   more _____
   label

Comparison Story Problem Strategies **219**

Name _____

Going Further

Vocabulary
table

Complete the **table**.

Then use the table to answer the question.

1.

Bicycles	1	2	3	4	5	6
Wheels	2	4	6	8		

bicycle

How many wheels are on 6 bicycles? [ ]

label

2.

Vases	1	2	3	4	5
Flowers	3	6	9		

vase

How many flowers are in 5 vases? [ ]

label

3.

People	1	2	3	4	5	6	7
Toes	10	20	30	40			

toes

How many toes do 7 people have? [ ]

label

Comparison Story Problem Strategies

Class Activity

Name _____

Vocabulary

measure   longest
long   shortest
inches

Measure the ribbons with Stair Steps.

1. Yellow ribbon   How **long**? _____ **inches**

2. Red ribbon   How long? _____ inches

3. Blue ribbon   How long? _____ inches

4. Green ribbon   How long? _____ inches

5. What color ribbon is the **longest**? _____

6. What color ribbon is the **shortest**? _____

Class Activity

Name _____

Vocabulary
measure
inches

Measure how far each ladybug walked.

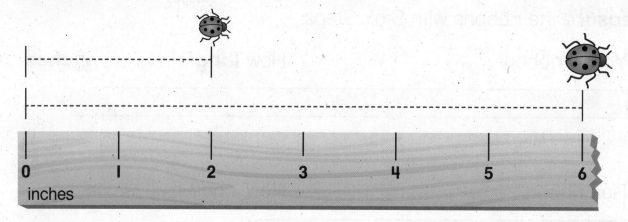

inches

1. Little ladybug   How far? _____ **inches**

2. Big ladybug   How far? _____ inches

Measure the bracelets.

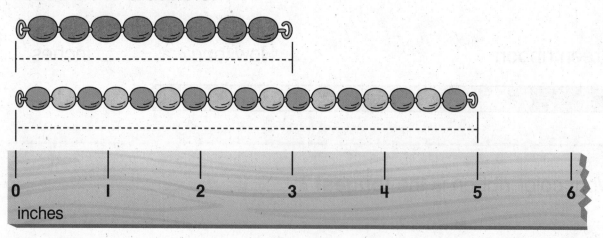

inches

3. Short bracelet   How long? _____ inches

4. Long bracelet   How long? _____ inches

Measurement with Inches

Class Activity

Name _____

Vocabulary
measure   shorter
table   longer
length

1. **Measure** the school supplies.
   Make a **table** of **lengths**.

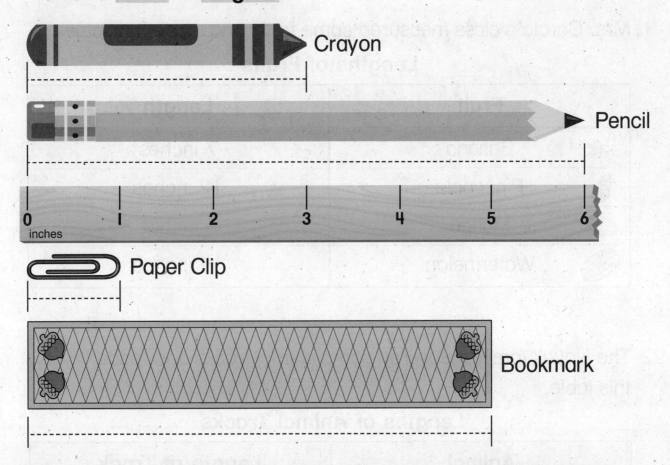

Crayon

Pencil

0 1 2 3 4 5 6
inches

Paper Clip

Bookmark

Object	Length
Crayon	
Pencil	
Paper Clip	
Bookmark	

2. How much **shorter** is the crayon than the pencil?

_____

3. How much **longer** is the bookmark than the paper clip?

Name

Class Activity

Ask questions about each table.

Use the words **longer** and **shorter**.

1. Mrs. Garcia's class measured some fruits and made this table.

Lengths of Fruits

	Fruit	Length
	Banana	7 inches
	Pineapple	12 inches
	Mango	5 inches
	Watermelon	14 inches

2. The Novak family measured some animal tracks and made this table.

Lengths of Animal Tracks

	Animal	Length of Track
	Squirrel	2 inches
	Deer	4 inches
	Raccoon	3 inches
	Moose	6 inches

Measurement Tables

Going Further

1. **Measure** the lines in inches.
   Make a **table** of distances.

Distances Between Animals

Animals	Distances
Lion to Elephant	
Lion to Dolphin	
Lion to Monkey	

2. **On the Back** Is the elephant or the monkey
   closer to the lion? Use words and numbers to explain.

Name _____

Measurement Tables

6-12

Class Activity

Name _____

Vocabulary
shape

Draw the next **shape** in each row.

1.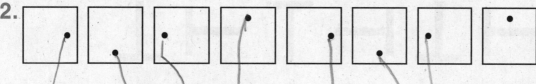

2.

3.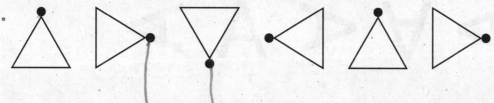

4.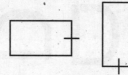
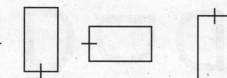

5.

6.

Extra Practice

Name _____

Vocabulary
turn

Draw the next letter in each row.

1. L ┌ ┐ ⌐ ⌐ ⌐

2. T ┤ ⊥ ├ ┬ ┤ ⊥

3. H I H I H I

4. D ⋃ ⋂ D ⋃ ⋂ D ⋃ ⋂ D ⋃ ⋂

5. A ▷ ▽ ◁ A ▷

6. Trace the letter P. **Turn** it.
   Draw what it looks like. Draw 5 more turns.

   P

Comparison and Rotation of Shapes

Class Activity

Class Activity

Name _____

Vocabulary
sort

1. **Sort** the shapes into two groups: shapes with corners and shapes with no corners. Draw each shape in the correct circle.

Shapes

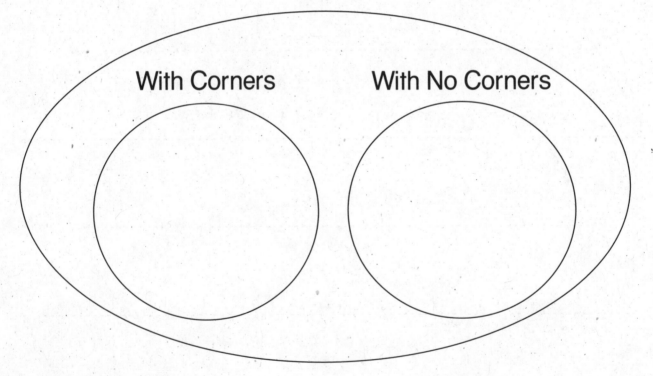

With Corners

With No Corners

2. Draw one more shape in each circle.

Shape Combinations

Name _____

Going Further

Draw a line to match like shapes.
Write the name of the shape.

Vocabulary
sphere
cube
cone
cylinder
rectangular prism

1. _____

2.   _____

3.  _____

4. _____

5.  _____

6. **On the Back** Think of an example of
a solid shape you have seen at home. What
is the object? What kind of solid shape is it?

Congruence and Solid Shapes **233**

Congruence and Solid Shapes

Class Activity

Name _____

Vocabulary

sorting rule
roll
stack
slide

Circle the solid shapes that follow the **sorting rule**.

1. Solid shapes that **roll**

2. Solid shapes that **stack**

3. Solid shapes that **slide**

4. Write your own sorting rule. Then circle the solid shapes that follow the rule.

My Sorting Rule _____

5. **On the Back** Choose 2 solid shapes.
   Tell how they are the same.

Name _____

Vocabulary
cone
cube
cylinder
sphere

Write the name of the two solid shapes in the picture.

1. _____

_____

2. 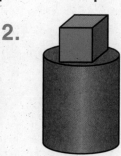 _____

_____

Predict how many cubes you need to build each shape. Then build the shape. Record the actual number of cubes you used.

3.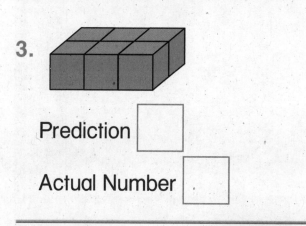

Prediction ☐

Actual Number ☐

4.

Prediction ☐

Actual Number ☐

5. Predict how many 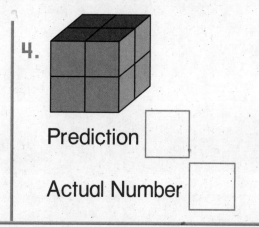 you can make from this shape. Then find the actual number.

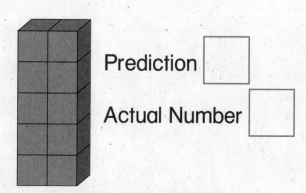   Prediction ☐

Actual Number ☐

6. **On the Back** Use cubes to build a shape.
   Then draw your shape.

Name

Exploration of Solid Shapes

Class Activity

Vocabulary

growing pattern

Continue each **growing pattern** two more times.

1.

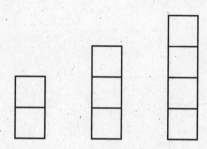

2.

3. AB ABB ABBB

4.
$$454$$
$$44544$$
$$4445444$$

Find the pattern and complete the table. Solve.

1.

Weeks	1	2		
Books	5	10		

Mina reads 5 books each week.
How many books will she read
in 4 weeks?

□ _____
label

2.

Months	1					
Dimes	10					

Corey's grandmother gives him 10
dimes each month. How many dimes
will he have after 6 months?

□ _____
label

3.

Days						
Miles						

Sam walks 3 miles each day.
How many miles does he walk
in 1 week?

□ _____
label

Name _____

Toys at the Toy Store

Balls	
Bears	
Cars	

Use the graph to answer the questions below.

1. Are there more balls or cars? _____

2. Are there fewer cars or bears? _____

3. The store has the most of which toy? _____

_____

4. Make a picture graph about the shapes.

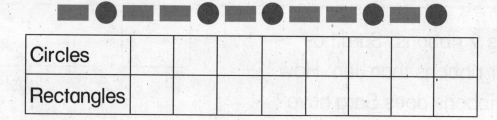

Circles							
Rectangles							

5. Complete the sentences. Ring the word **more** or **fewer**.

There are [ ] **more** **fewer** rectangles than circles.

There are [ ] **more** **fewer** circles than rectangles.

Name _____

Solve the story problems.
Use drawings and numbers.

---

6. Terry made 8 pictures. Sanjay made 4 more than Terry. How many pictures did Sanjay make?

□ _____
label

---

7. Maya has 7 pears. Raul has 4 pears. How many fewer pears does Raul have than Maya?

□ _____
label

---

8. Jen has 9 ribbons. Sara has 6 fewer ribbons than Jen. How many ribbons does Sara have?

□ _____
label

---

9. Ms. Patel has 12 plants. Mr. Jones has 7 plants. How many more plants does Ms. Patel have than Mr. Jones?

□ _____
label

Solve the story problems.
Use drawings and numbers.

---

10. There were 18 rabbits yesterday.
    There are 5 fewer today.
    How many are there today?

    ☐ , _____
    label

---

11. Matt has 9 flowers. Olga has
    5 flowers. How many more flowers
    does Matt have than Olga?

    ☐ _____
    label

---

12. Make a table from the picture graph below.

Picture Graph

Zebras	🦓 🦓 🦓 🦓
Camels	🐪 🐪 🐪 🐪 🐪
Lions	🦁 🦁 🦁

Table

Animal	Number

13. How many zebras are there? _____

14. Are there more lions or camels? _____

15. Are there fewer lions or zebras? _____

16. Measure the school supplies. Complete the table.

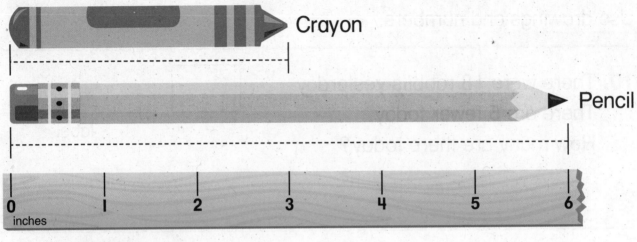

Crayon

Pencil

0 1 2 3 4 5 6
inches

Eraser

Object	Length
Crayon	
Pencil	
Eraser	

17. How much shorter is the crayon than the pencil? _____ inches

18. How much longer is the pencil than the eraser? _____ inches

19. How much shorter is the eraser than the crayon? _____ inch

20. Extended Response Use the table. Write and answer a question to compare length.

_____

_____

Dear Family:

In math class, children will begin to explore common fractions and the relationship between parts and the whole. They will develop strategies for finding one half and one fourth of a number. They will also find fractional parts of a set of objects, using trial and error methods.

For example, children will find halves and fourths of common geometric shapes, such as a rectangle.

$\frac{1}{2}$ $\frac{1}{4}$

Later in the unit, children will extend their understanding of fractions to include halves and fourths of 100 as numbers and as coins (half dollar and quarter).

Further applications of wholes and halves are seen when clocks and time are discussed. Children are introduced to digital and analog clocks. They learn to tell time in whole- and half-hours.

Finally, children begin investigating simple circle graphs. They will use such graphs to make comparisons. They will also convert information on a graph to a table.

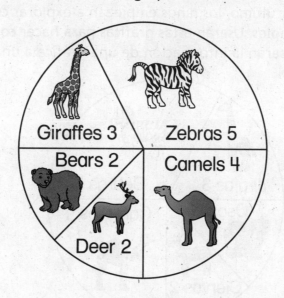

Giraffes	3
Zebras	5
Bears	2
Deer	2
Camels	4
Total	16

Sincerely,
Your child's teacher

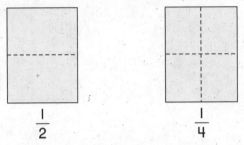

Carta a la familia

Estimada familia:

En la clase de matemáticas los niños van a empezar a explorar las fracciones comunes y la relación entre las partes y el todo. Van a desarrollar estrategias para hallar una mitad y un cuarto de un número. Hallarán también las partes fraccionarias de un conjunto de objetos, usando métodos de prueba y error.

Por ejemplo, los niños hallarán las mitades y los cuartos de figuras geométricas comunes, como los rectángulos.

$$\frac{1}{2} \qquad \frac{1}{4}$$

Más adelante en la unidad los niños van a ampliar su comprensión de las fracciones al incluir las mitades y los cuartos de 100. Más adelante en la unidad los niños van a ampliar su comprensión de las fracciones al incluir las mitades y los cuartos de 100, tanto en forma de número como de monedas (monedas de 50 centavos y monedas de 25 centavos).

Verán más aplicaciones de los todos y las mitades cuando estudien los relojes y la hora. Los niños llegan a conocer los relojes analógicos y digitales. Aprenden a decir las horas enteras y las medias.

Por último, los niños empiezan a explorar con gráficas circulares simples. Usarán estas gráficas para hacer comparaciones. También pasarán la información de una gráfica a una tabla.

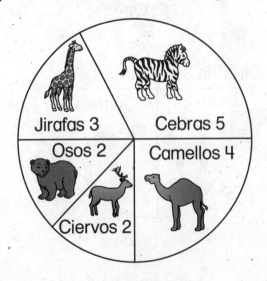

Jirafas	3
Cebras	5
Osos	2
Ciervos	2
Camellos	4
Total	16

Atentamente,
El maestro de su niño

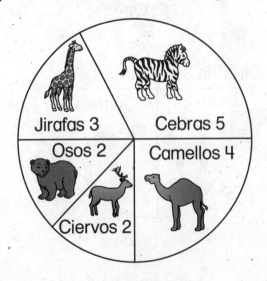

Investigate Doubles

Going Further

Name _____

Vocabulary
double

Find the **double**.

1. 3 + 3 = ☐   2. 4 + 4 = ☐   3. 5 + 5 = ☐

4. 6 + 6 = ☐   5. 7 + 7 = ☐   6. 8 + 8 = ☐

7. 9 + 9 = ☐   8. 10 + 10 = ☐

Use doubles to find the total.

9. 3 + 4 = ☐   10. 5 + 4 = ☐   11. 6 + 5 = ☐

12. 6 + 7 = ☐   13. 7 + 8 = ☐   14. 9 + 8 = ☐

15. 9 + 10 = ☐   16. 10 + 11 = ☐   17. 7 + 6 = ☐

18. 4 + 5 = ☐   19. 5 + 6 = ☐   20. 8 + 7 = ☐

🔄 21. **On the Back** Look back at Exercises 9–20. Choose 2 problems. Explain how you found the total.

Problem Solve with Doubles

Extra Practice

1. Make **half** the recipe. Write the amount for each ingredient.

Half	A Recipe for Playdough
	6 cups flour
	12 cups oatmeal
	6 cups water

2. **Double** the recipe. Write the amount for each ingredient.

Double	A Recipe for Play Clay
	4 cups cornstarch
	3 cups white glue
	7 drops food coloring

3. Draw 10 crackers. Ring half of them.

Extra Practice

1. Use doubles to add.

$3 + 3 =$ ☐ $7 + 7 =$ ☐ $1 + 1 =$ ☐

$8 + 8 =$ ☐ $5 + 5 =$ ☐ $4 + 4 =$ ☐

$4 + 4 =$ ☐ $9 + 9 =$ ☐ $7 + 7 =$ ☐

$6 + 6 =$ ☐ $3 + 3 =$ ☐ $5 + 5 =$ ☐

$2 + 2 =$ ☐ $8 + 8 =$ ☐ $9 + 9 =$ ☐

2. Use halves to subtract.

$6 - 3 =$ ☐ $2 - 1 =$ ☐ $4 - 2 =$ ☐

$12 - 6 =$ ☐ $8 - 4 =$ ☐ $10 - 5 =$ ☐

$16 - 8 =$ ☐ $14 - 7 =$ ☐ $18 - 9 =$ ☐

The Meaning of Half

Class Activity

Cut out the shapes below.

How many ways can you fold them in half?

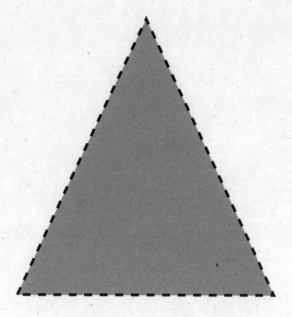

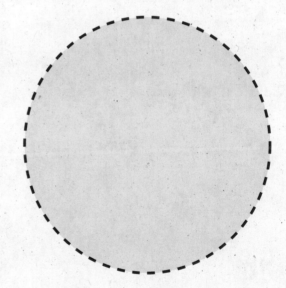

Symmetrical Shapes

Going Further

1. Decorate the butterfly kite.
   Make each **half** the same.

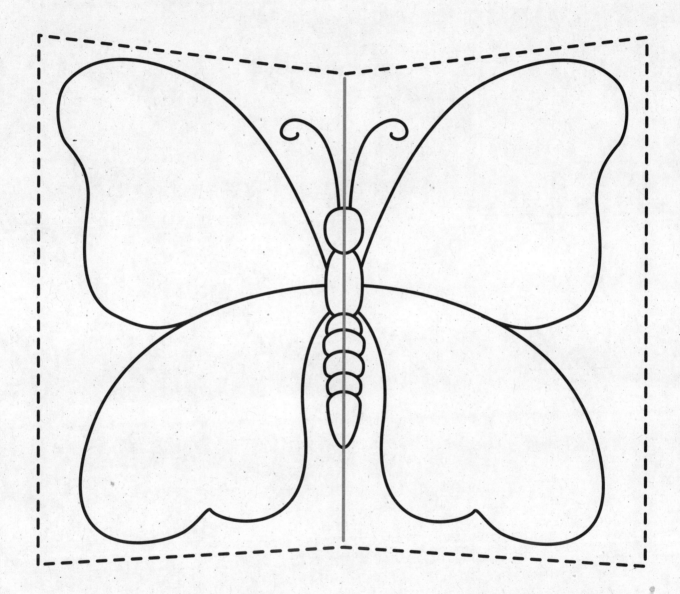

2. Fold along the middle line.
   Then cut on the outside dashed line.

Half of a Shape and Symmetry

Name _____

Class Activity

Vocabulary

one fourth
quarter

1. Ring **one fourth** of a dollar (100 pennies).

2. How many cents?

Total so far _____ _____ _____

3. **Show** Ring the pennies in Exercise 1 to show
   the value of three **quarters**.

Going Further

Solve the story problems.

1. Four friends want to share a sandwich. How should they cut the sandwich so that each child gets the same amount? Draw lines to show the equal shares. Color each share a different color.

2. The 4 friends want to share a pie for dessert. How should they cut the pie so that each child gets the same size slice? Draw lines to show the equal shares. Color each share a different color.

3. One friend wants only half of her pie slice. How should she cut her slice in half? Draw a line to show the halves. Color each half a different color.

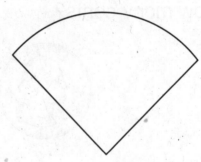

Class Activity

Color the fraction strips. Cut on the dashed lines.

Color
1 whole.

1 whole

Color $\frac{1}{2}$.

$\frac{1}{2}$	$\frac{1}{2}$

Color $\frac{1}{3}$.

$\frac{1}{3}$	$\frac{1}{3}$	$\frac{1}{3}$

Color $\frac{1}{4}$.

$\frac{1}{4}$	$\frac{1}{4}$	$\frac{1}{4}$	$\frac{1}{4}$

Color $\frac{1}{5}$.

$\frac{1}{5}$	$\frac{1}{5}$	$\frac{1}{5}$	$\frac{1}{5}$	$\frac{1}{5}$

Color $\frac{1}{6}$.

$\frac{1}{6}$	$\frac{1}{6}$	$\frac{1}{6}$	$\frac{1}{6}$	$\frac{1}{6}$	$\frac{1}{6}$

Class Activity

Vocabulary
circle graph
fraction

The **circle graphs** on this page show what 3 children did with a dollar.

Tim

Snack | Pencil
Toy | Save

1. How many cents did Tim save?

   _____¢

2. What **fraction** of the dollar did Tim spend on the snack and the pencil together?

   _____

Jamila

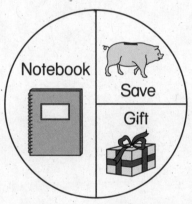

Notebook | Save
Gift

3. How many cents did Jamila spend on the notebook? _____¢

4. What fraction of the dollar did Jamila save?

   _____

Kelly

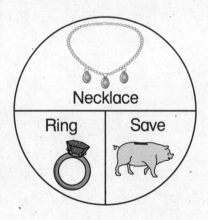

Necklace
Ring | Save

5. Kelly spent twice as much money on the _____ as on the ring.

6. What fraction of the dollar did Kelly save? _____

➡ 7. **On the Back** Show 50¢, 25¢, and 25¢ on a circle graph of one dollar.

Introduction to Circle Graphs and Probability

Class Activity

Animals at the Zoo

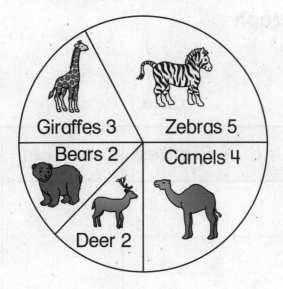

1. The zoo has the most of which animal? _____

2. How many more camels are there than bears? _____

3. How many fewer deer are there than zebras? _____

4. There are the same number of _____ and _____.

Rows of Vegetables in the Garden

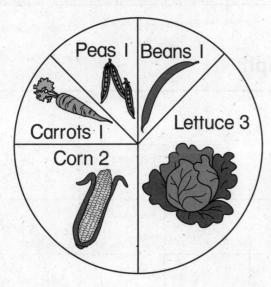

5. How many more rows of lettuce are there than rows of carrots?

_____

6. How many fewer rows of peas are there than rows of corn?

_____

7. The garden has the most of which vegetable?

_____

8. How many rows of vegetables are there altogether? _____

Class Activity

Name _____

Vocabulary
circle graph
picture graph

Make a table of the clothes that are in the **circle graph**. Then make a **picture graph** with the same information.

Clothes in the Closet

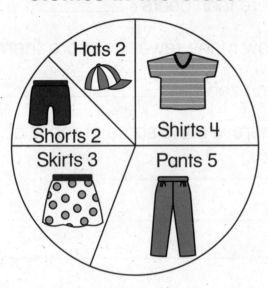

Hats 2
Shirts 4
Shorts 2
Skirts 3
Pants 5

1. ## Table

Kind of Clothes	Number

2. ## Picture Graph

Comparisons with Circle Graphs

Going Further

Each graph has a total of 12 animals. Find the unknown number of animals on each graph.

1. **Pets**

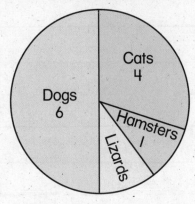

How many lizards?

☐ _____

label

2. **Sea Mammals**

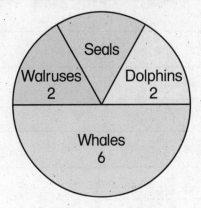

How many seals?

☐ _____

label

3. **Forest Animals**

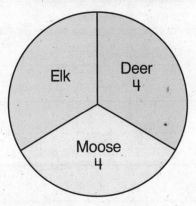

How many elk?

☐ _____

label

4. **Big Cats**

How many tigers?

☐ _____

label

➡ **5. On the Back** Write a comparison question based on one of the graphs. Then answer your question.

Comparisons with Circle Graphs

Class Activity

Fill in the numbers on the clock.
Attach the clock hands.

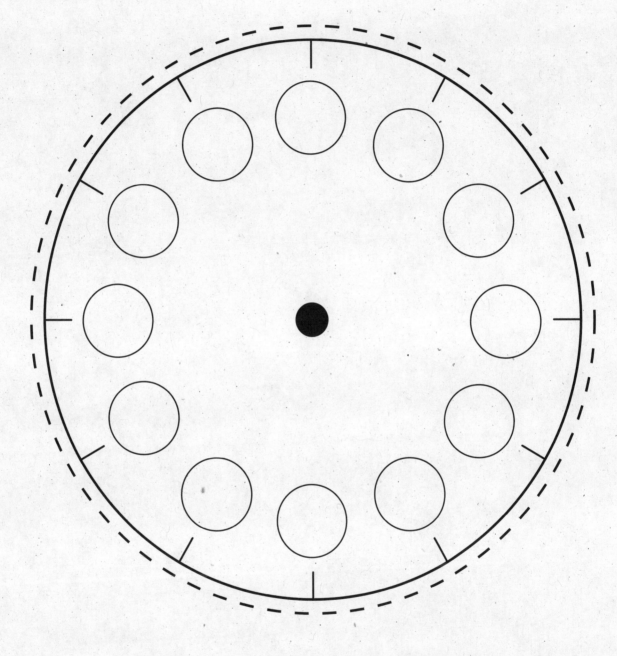

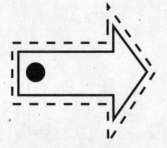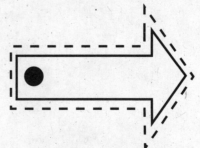

Class Activity

Name

1.

[:]

2.

[:]

3.

[:]

4.

5.

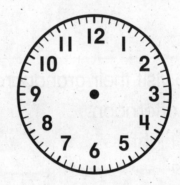

6.

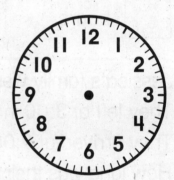

7.

[:]

8.

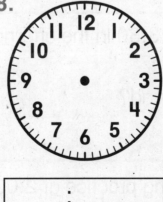

[:]

9.

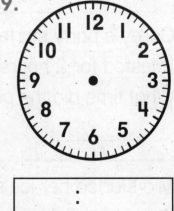

[:]

Going Further

Name _____

Solve the story problems. Use a clock.

1. The football game started at 1:00 in the
   afternoon. It ended at 4:00 in the afternoon.
   How long did the game last?

   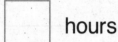 hours

2. Tony went to the park at 10:00 in the morning.
   He played until his lunchtime at 12:00.
   How long did Tony play at the park?

   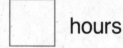 hours

3. Jessica's family went to visit their grandparents.
   They left at 3:00 in the afternoon.
   They arrived at 9:00 at night.
   How long was their trip?

   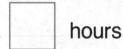 hours

4. Corey's party started at 3:30 in the afternoon.
   It lasted for 2 hours.
   What time did the party end?

   _____

5. Mio started her ice skating practice at 2:00.
   She practiced for 1 hour 30 minutes.
   What time did she finish practicing?

Tell Time to the Half-Hour

Class Activity

Name _____

Use the **table** to make a **circle graph** and a **picture graph**.

Kind of Cereal	Number
oatmeal	3
flakes	6
granola	3

Circle Graph

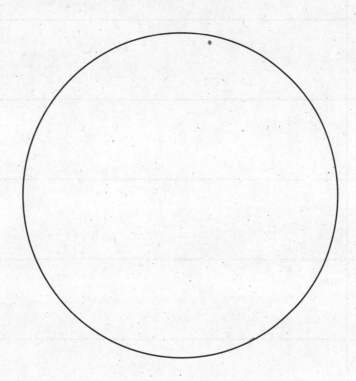

Picture Graph

Kind of Cereal	Number				

Consolidation: Clocks and Graphs **269**

Class Activity

School-Day Schedule

Name _____

Extra Practice

Each show lasts 30 minutes. You can walk from one show to another in less than 30 minutes.

Bird House

Shows at:
11:00, 1:00, 3:00

Petting Zoo

Open All Day

African Savannah

Shows at:
11:00, 1:00, 2:00, 3:00

Cafeteria

Open All Day

Jungle Adventure

Shows at:
11:00, 1:00, 2:00, 3:00

American Forest

Open All Day

Arctic World

Shows at:
11:00, 1:00, 3:00

Reptile House

Shows at:
11:00, 1:00, 3:00

Plan a day at the zoo. Use the posters. Choose the things you would like to do. Fill in the schedule.

10:00–11:00	11:00–12:00	12:00–1:00	1:00–2:00	2:00–3:00	3:00–4:00

⬤ **On the Back** Use your schedule to write a question. Then answer your question.

Consolidation: Clocks and Graphs

Fill in the calendar for this month.

Month of _____

Sunday	Monday	Tuesday	Wednesday	Thursday	Friday	Saturday

Use the calendar to find the answer.

1. What day of the week is today? _____

2. What day of the week is tomorrow? _____

3. What day of the week was yesterday? _____

4. What day of the week is the fifth? _____

5. What is the date of the second Sunday in this month?

   _____

6. If today is the tenth, what day of the week is tomorrow?

   _____

7. What is the date of the first Friday in this month?

   _____

8. What day of the week comes after the last date on your calendar? _____

Class Activity

Name _____

Use the calendars to answer the questions.

June						
Sun.	Mon.	Tues.	Wed.	Thurs.	Fri.	Sat.
					1	2
3	4	5	6	7	8	9
10	11	12	13	14	15	16
17	18	19	20	21	22	23
24	25	26	27	28	29	30

July						
Sun.	Mon.	Tues.	Wed.	Thurs.	Fri.	Sat.
1	2	3	4	5	6	7
8	9	10	11	12	13	14
15	16	17	18	19	20	21
22	23	24	25	26	27	28
29	30	31				

August						
Sun.	Mon.	Tues.	Wed.	Thurs.	Fri.	Sat.
			1	2	3	4
5	6	7	8	9	10	11
12	13	14	15	16	17	18
19	20	21	22	23	24	25
26	27	28	29	30	31	

1. Which of these months has the fewest number of days? _____

2. Which month has 5 Thursdays? _____

3. Make an X on the Fourth of July.

4. Ring all the Mondays in August.

5. What month comes before June? _____

6. Choose a month. Draw a picture of something you like to do that month.

Calendars and Units of Time

Name _____

Lupe and Kavi wrote these reports for their Science Fair projects. They both planted 4 lima bean seeds about 6 weeks ago.

Lupe's Report	Kavi's Report
All 4 seeds sprouted. They are growing. I measured them today. Plant 1: 6 inches Plant 2: 5 inches Plant 3: 6 inches Plant 4: 4 inches	All 4 seeds sprouted. It took 2 weeks for them to sprout. Now they are growing between 1 and 2 inches every week. I measure them every week.

	W1	W2	W3	W4	W5	W6
P1	0	0	1	2	3	4
P2	0	0	2	3	5	6
P3	0	0	2	4	5	6
P4	0	1	2	3	4	5

P = Plant   W = Week

1. What does Lupe's report tell you?

_____

_____

2. What does Kavi's report tell you?

_____

_____

3. Whose report tells more about the way beans grow? Explain your answer.

_____

_____

When does a flip look the same as a slide?
First, cut out the shapes that your teacher gives you.
Then, draw a vertical line on a piece of paper.

1. Flip Shape A over the vertical line.

   Draw what it looks like before and after the flip.

2. Slide Shape A across the vertical line.

   Draw what it looks like before and after the slide.

3. Do the flip and slide of Shape A look the same or different? Ring the answer.   Same   Different

4. Flip Shape B over the vertical line.

   Draw what happens.

5. Slide Shape B across the vertical line.

   Draw what happens.

6. Do the flip and slide of Shape B look the same or different? Ring the answer.   Same   Different

7. Flip and slide the other shapes. Draw what happens.

8. When does a flip look the same as a slide?

   _____

   _____

Use Mathematical Processes

Use doubles to add.

1.

$6 + 6 = $ ⬚

2.

$7 + 7 = $ ⬚

3.

$9 + 9 = $ ⬚

4.

$8 + 8 = $ ⬚

Make each rectangle twice as big.

5.

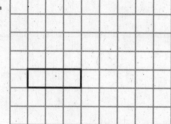

6.

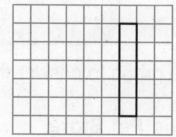

How much is shaded? Write $\frac{1}{2}$ or $\frac{1}{4}$.

7.

_____

8.

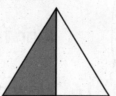

_____

9.

_____

Ring half of the objects. Then fill in the blanks.

10.    Half of ____ is ____.

11.    Half of ____ is ____.

Ring one fourth of the objects. Then fill in the blanks.

12. ████ ████ ████ ████   One fourth of ____ is ____.

13. ◡◡◡◡ ◡◡◡◡   One fourth of ____ is ____.

Use the circle graph to answer the questions.

Pets at the Pet Store

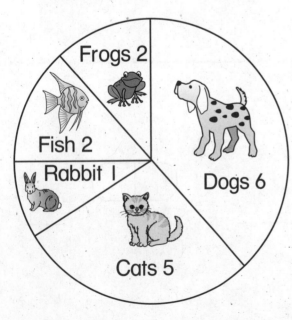

14. The pet store has the most of which pet? _____

15. How many more cats are there than frogs? _____

16. How many fewer fish are there than dogs? _____

Write the time in the boxes.

17.

| : |

18.

| : |

19. Ring the month that comes before April.

August

March

May

20. **Extended Response** Write an equation with doubles and a teen total. Make a drawing of the doubles.

Class Activity

Vocabulary
dime
nickel
penny

Show the price with sticks and circles.
Then write how many of each coin.

1.

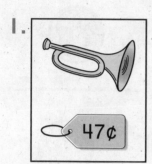

47¢

Dimes _____ **Nickels** _____ **Pennies** _____

2.

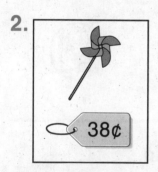

38¢

Dimes _____ Nickels _____ Pennies _____

3.

69¢

Dimes _____ Nickels _____ Pennies _____

4.

95¢

Dimes _____ Nickels _____ Pennies _____

Dimes, Nickels, and Pennies **281**

Ring the correct coin.

1. I am silver-colored.
   I am worth half a dime.
   What am I?

2. You need 10 of me
   to make a dime.
   What am I?

3. You can use two of me
   to make 20¢.
   What am I?

Read the amount. Write the name of the unknown coin.

4. 47¢

    _____

5. 60¢

   _____

6. 28¢

    _____

Dimes, Nickels, and Pennies

Dear Family:

In the current math unit, children are learning to use coins in different combinations to show a total number of cents. They use real quarters, dimes, nickels, and pennies to calculate totals and identify alternate coin combinations. Children are also learning how to convert cents into coins and to convert coins into cents.

There are several ways children can identify an amount of money shown by coins. One method is to use stick-and-circle drawings in which each stick represents 10¢ and each circle represents 1¢. Children use these drawings to represent the coins in story problems, circling each 5-group to make a nickel. For example:

Sonya has 4 dimes, 1 nickel, and 3 pennies. How much money does she have?

| | | | ⬭⬭⬭⬭⬭   ooo   **48¢**

<u>4</u> dimes   <u>1</u> nickel   <u>3</u> pennies

Children can solve the same problem by converting the coins to cents, and then building and solving an equation.

$$10¢ + 10¢ + 10¢ + 10¢ + 5¢ + 3¢ = 48¢$$

Your child's work with coin conversions will help him or her proceed smoothly to later lessons in the unit, during which children will explore multi-digit addition strategies.

Sincerely,
Your child's teacher

Carta a la familia

Estimada familia:

En esta unidad, los niños aprenden a usar monedas en diferentes combinaciones para mostrar el total en centavos. Utilizan monedas reales de veinticinco, diez, cinco y un centavos para calcular los totales e identificar varias combinaciones posibles de monedas. Los niños también están aprendiendo a transformar centavos en monedas y transformar monedas en centavos.

Hay varias maneras en que los niños pueden identificar una cantidad de dinero con monedas. Un método es usar dibujos de palitos y círculos en los que cada palito representa 10¢ y cada círculo representa 1¢. Los niños usan estos dibujos para representar las monedas en problemas, rodeando con un círculo cada grupo de cinco para formar una moneda de cinco centavos. Por ejemplo:

Sonya tiene 4 monedas de 10 centavos, 1 de cinco centavos y 3 de un centavo. ¿Cuánto dinero tiene?

| | | | ⬭ooooo⬭   ooo   **48¢**

<u>4</u> monedas de 10¢   <u>1</u> moneda de 5¢   <u>3</u> monedas de 1¢

Los niños pueden resolver el mismo problema transformando las monedas a centavos y luego formando y resolviendo una ecuación.

$$10¢ + 10¢ + 10¢ + 10¢ + 5¢ + 3¢ = 48¢$$

El trabajo con la conversión de monedas ayudará a su niño a pasar sin demasiada dificultad a otras lecciones de la unidad en las que van a explorar métodos para la suma con números de varios dígitos.

Atentamente,
El maestro de su niño

Dimes, Nickels, and Pennies

Name _____

Going Further

Write the value of the coins. Ring the two boxes that have the same amount.

1.

_____

2.

_____

3.

_____

4.

_____

5.

_____

6.

_____

7. **On the Back** Show 4 different sets of coins that have the same value as the coins in Exercise 5.

Find Equivalent Coins and Values

How much for each pair of things?

1.  +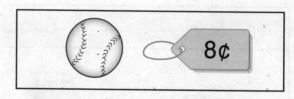

☐ ¢

2.  +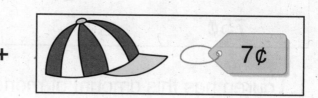

☐ ¢

3. 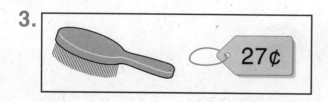 +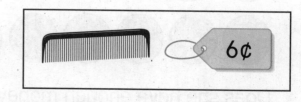

☐ ¢

4. +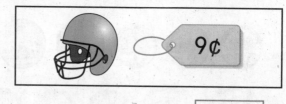

☐ ¢

5. 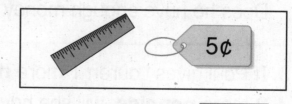 +

☐ ¢

Extra Practice

Name _____

Vocabulary
nickel
penny

Use the menu to answer the questions.

Snack Bar Menu

75¢   45¢   60¢   50¢

1. Lauren has this amount of money:

Does she have enough money to buy a banana?   Yes ☐   No ☐

2. Paul has this amount of money:

Does he have enough money to buy an apple?   Yes ☐   No ☐

3. If Paul gives Lauren 1 more **nickel** and
   2 more **pennies**, will she have enough money
   to buy a bottle of juice?   Yes ☐   No ☐

Make Coin Conversions

Name

28 apples

16 apples

Uncle David
28 Apples

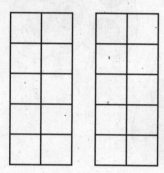

_____

Put extra apples here.

Aunt Sarah
16 Apples

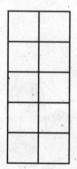

_____

Put extra apples here.

Total Apples

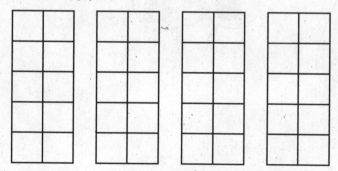

_____

Put extra apples here.

Going Further

Name

Find the total number of berries.

Total: [   ] berries

Explore Multi-Digit Addition

Dear Family:

Your child has been using special drawings of 10-sticks and circles to add greater numbers. The sticks show the number of tens, and the circles show the number of ones. When a new group of ten is made, it is circled.

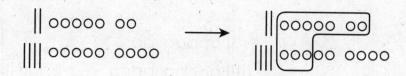

There are several ways for children to show the new group of ten when they add with numbers.

1. Children can do the addition with a **single total.** The 1 for the new ten can be written either below the tens column or above it. Writing it below makes addition easier because the 1 new ten is added after children have added the two numbers that are already there. Also, children can see the 16 they made from 7 and 9 because the 1 and 6 are closer together than they were when the new ten was written above.

$$\begin{array}{r} 27 \\ +\ 49 \\ \underline{1} \\ 76 \end{array}$$ new ten below

$$\begin{array}{r} 1 \\ 27 \\ +\ 49 \\ \hline 76 \end{array}$$ new ten above

2. Children can make **separate totals** for tens and ones. Many first-graders prefer to work from left to right because that is how they read. They add the tens (20 + 40 = 60) and then the ones (7 + 9 = 16). The last step is to add the two totals together (60 + 16 = 76).

$$\begin{array}{r} 27 \\ +\ 49 \\ \hline 60 \\ +\ 16 \\ \hline 76 \end{array}$$
left to right

$$\begin{array}{r} 27 \\ +\ 49 \\ \hline 16 \\ +\ 60 \\ \hline 76 \end{array}$$
right to left

You may notice your child using one of these methods as he or she completes homework.

Sincerely,
Your child's teacher

Estimada familia:

Su niño ha estado usando dibujos especiales de palitos de 10 y círculos para sumar números más grandes. Los palitos muestran el número de decenas y los círculos muestran el número de unidades. Cuando se forma un nuevo grupo de diez, se hace un círculo a su alrededor.

Existen varias maneras de que los niños muestren el nuevo grupo de diez cuando suman números.

1. Los niños pueden hacer la suma con un **total único.** El 1 que indica la nueva decena se puede escribir abajo o arriba de la columna de las decenas. Escribirlo abajo hace que la suma sea más fácil porque la nueva decena se suma después de que los niños hayan sumado los dos números que ya estaban allí. Además, los niños pueden ver el 16 que obtuvieron de 7 y 9 porque el 1 y el 6 están más cerca uno de otro que cuando la nueva decena estaba escrita arriba.

$$\begin{array}{r} 27 \\ +49 \\ \underline{1} \\ 76 \end{array}$$ nueva decena abajo

$$\begin{array}{r} 1 \\ 27 \\ +49 \\ \hline 76 \end{array}$$ nueva decena arriba

2. Los niños pueden hacer **totales separados** para decenas y para unidades. Muchos estudiantes de primer grado prefieren trabajar de izquierda a derecha porque esa es la manera en que leen. Suman las decenas (20 + 40 = 60) y luego las unidades (7 + 9 = 16). El último paso es sumar ambos totales (60 + 16 = 76).

$$\begin{array}{r} 27 \\ +49 \\ \hline 60 \\ +16 \\ \hline 76 \end{array}$$

de izquierda a derecha

$$\begin{array}{r} 27 \\ +49 \\ \hline 16 \\ +60 \\ \hline 76 \end{array}$$

de derecha a izquierda

Es posible que Ud. observe que su niño usa uno de estos métodos al hacer la tarea.

Atentamente,
El maestro de su niño

Explore Multi-Digit Addition

Name

1. Work in pairs. Each child chooses one apple tree.

2. On your MathBoard or paper, add the apples in the two trees.

3. Check to see if you both got the same answer.

4. Repeat with other trees.

5. **On the Back** Choose one of the trees above. Write a story problem with that number and the number 18. Then solve the problem.

Name

Student Methods: 2-Digit Addition

28
peaches

42
peaches

35
peaches

48
peaches

47
peaches

50
peaches

16
peaches

49
peaches

27
peaches

43
peaches

1. Work in pairs. Each child chooses one peach tree.

2. On your MathBoard or paper, add the peaches in the two trees.

3. Check to see if you both got the same answer.

4. Repeat with other trees.

5. **On the Back** Write 3 problems that will make a new ten.
   Write or draw how you chose them.

Discuss Solution Methods: 2-Digit Addition

Class Activity

Name _____

Solve the story problems.

Show your work. Use drawings, numbers, or words.

1. Arturo grew 35 melons this year and 48 melons last year. How many melons did he grow in all?

melon

☐ _____
label

2. I saw 18 yellow butterflies and 29 white ones. What was the total number of butterflies I saw?

butterfly

☐ _____
label

3. We found 26 maple leaves and 45 oak leaves in the forest. How many leaves did we find altogether?

forest

☐ _____
label

➡ 4. **On the Back** Write an addition story problem about 27 apples and 64 apples. Solve it.

2-Digit Story Problems

Fruit and Vegetable Stand

Peach 36¢

Celery 49¢

Pear 38¢

Grapes 50¢

Apple 24¢

Beans 35¢

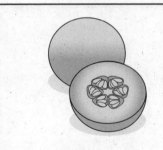

Melon 46¢

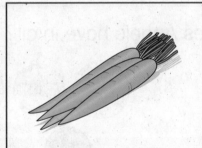

Carrots 47¢

Pepper 20¢

Lettuce 39¢

Tomato 30¢

Cucumber 18¢

Going Further

Name _____

1. How much **money** does Stephen have in all?

         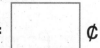

_____ ¢   +   _____ ¢   =   [   ] ¢

2. How much money does Ranjani have in all?

_____ ¢   +   _____ ¢   =   [   ] ¢

3. How much money does Angela have in all?

_____ ¢   +   _____ ¢   =   [   ] ¢

4. Ring the name of the person who has the most money.

Stephen   Ranjani   Angela

Real World Problems: 2-Digit Addition

Each child wants to buy a school pin.
The pins cost 80 cents.

Fill in the blanks. Then draw lines to match to the coins.

1. Josh has 64 cents.
   How much more money
   does he need?

   _____ cents more

2. Delia has 54 cents.
   How much more money
   does she need?

   _____ cents more

3. Eric has 58 cents.
   How much more money
   does he need?

   _____ cents more

4. Jackie has 74 cents.
   How much more money
   does she need?

   _____ cents more

5. **On the Back** Choose an amount between 20 cents
   and 30 cents. Pretend you have this much money.
   How much more do you need to buy a school pin?
   Draw the coins to show the amount.

2-Digit Addition: Unknown Partners

Name _____

Solve the story problems.
Use the Penny Arrays to help you.

---

1. Helen has 32 cents. She wants
to buy a basket that costs 1 dollar.
How much more does she need?

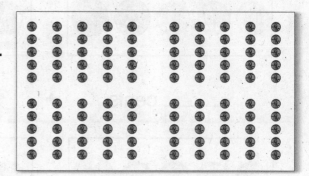

[   ] ¢

---

2. Paulo has 56 cents. He needs
1 dollar to go see the dolphins.
How much more does he need?

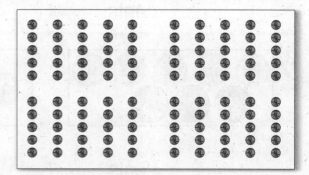

[   ] ¢

---

3. Jamaya has 49 cents. She
wants a box of crayons that
costs 1 dollar. How much more
does she need?

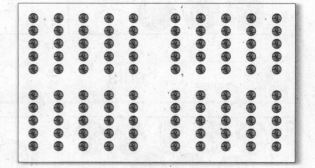

[   ] ¢

Going Further

Write the amount under each box.
Then add to find the total amount.

1.

_____ cents   +   _____ cents   =   _____ cents

2.

_____ cents   +   _____ cents   =   _____ cents

3.

_____ cents   +   _____ cents   =   _____ cents

4.

_____ cents   +   _____ cents   =   _____ cents

5.

_____ cents   +   _____ cents   =   _____ cents

Cut out the dollars. Use them for buying fruits and vegetables.

Dollar Bills

Name _____

Each item is paid for with 1 dollar.
Write the number of pennies, nickels, or dimes you need
to make change.
Then write the total change.

	Spend	(penny)	(nickel)	(dime)	Total Change
1.	78¢				[ ] ¢
2.	83¢				[ ] ¢
3.	54¢				[ ] ¢
4.	47¢				[ ] ¢
5.	21¢				[ ] ¢

➡ **6. On the Back** Choose an amount
above. How did you find the change?
Write or draw to explain.

Make Change for a Dollar

Name _____

How many cents?

1.

10 10 10 5 1

 ¢

2.

___ ___ ___ ___ ___ ___ ___ ___ ___

 ¢

How much altogether? Solve with sticks and circles.

3.

34¢ + 4¢

▢ ¢

Add the numbers. Make a proof drawing with
sticks and circles. Did you make a new ten?

4. 64
  + 23
	5. 16
	  + 39

New ten? yes ☐ no ☐	New ten? yes ☐ no ☐

6. 57
  + 26
	7. 72
	  + 15

New ten? yes ☐ no ☐	New ten? yes ☐ no ☐

Solve the story problems.

Show your work. Use drawings, numbers, or words.

---

8. Jamie bought an orange for
2 dimes, 1 nickel, and 4 pennies.
How many cents did he pay?

orange

☐ ¢

---

9. Ruby has 4 dimes, 2 nickels,
and 7 pennies in her purse.
How many cents does she have?

purse

☐ ¢

---

10. Extended Response Add 48 and 25. Did you make a
new ten? Explain.

_____

_ _

_____

_ _

Class Activity

Vocabulary
unknown partner

1. Rosa read 8 stories. Tim read 5. How many did they read in all?

Rosa _____   Tim _____   In all _____

2. Rosa read 8 stories. Tim also read some stories. They read 13 stories in all. How many stories did Tim read?

Rosa _____   Tim _____   In all _____

3. Rosa read some stories. Tim read 5 stories. They read 13 stories in all. How many stories did Rosa read?

Rosa _____   Tim _____   In all _____

4. **On the Back** Write a teen story problem with an **unknown partner**. Solve it.

Teen Problems with Various Unknowns

Dear Family:

Your child has begun a unit that focuses on developing analytical skills in order to examine, classify, sort, and solve story problems.

Children will analyze and solve story problems with various unknowns, using counting on, the Make a Ten strategy, and numeric methods. Although stick-and-circle drawings continue to be acceptable, children should begin to use numeric methods (such as New Group Below) more frequently as they grow more comfortable with the concept of place value.

For the first time, children will be asked to solve story problems involving items that are different, yet fall under the same category. Recognizing "unlike terms" will sharpen children's logical awareness and classification skills, as well as expose them to more vocabulary. The following is an example of a category story problem:

At the petting zoo, Amanda fed four goats. Then she fed two lambs. How many animals did she feed in all?

Once children are familiar with category story problems, they will begin to differentiate between important information for solving the problem and irrelevant information. The following is an example of a story problem with extra information:

Jorge read six books and eight magazines last month. He read nine more books this month. How many books has Jorge read altogether?

As children learn to analyze story problems, they will also create their own problems using skills they acquire in each lesson. These original story problems will be shared and solved during the Story Problem Festival at the end of the unit.

If you have any questions, please do not hesitate to contact me.

Sincerely,
Your child's teacher

Carta a la familia

Estimada familia:

Su niño ha empezado una unidad que trata del desarrollo de destrezas analíticas para estudiar, clasificar, ordenar y resolver problemas.

Los niños analizarán y resolverán problemas con varias partes desconocidas. Pueden contar hacia adelante, usar la estrategia de hacer una decena o usar métodos numéricos. Aunque se aceptan los dibujos de círculos y palitos, los niños deben empezar a usar los métodos numéricos (como el de grupos nuevos abajo) con más frecuencia a medida que se sienten más cómodos con el concepto del valor posicional.

Por primera vez, se les pedirá que resuelvan problemas que tengan artículos diferentes, pero que pertenecen a la misma categoría. Identificar "términos no iguales" agudizará el conocimiento lógico de los niños y las destrezas de clasificación, además de que usarán vocabulario nuevo. El siguiente es un ejemplo de un problema de clasificación.

En el zoológico de mascotas, Amanda dio de comer a cuatro cabras. Después dio de comer a dos ovejas. ¿A cuántos animales dio de comer en total?

Una vez que los niños se han familiarizado con los problemas de clasificación empezarán a diferenciar entre la información que puede ayudarlos a responder lo que se les pregunta y la información que sobra. El siguiente es un ejemplo de un problema con información adicional:

Jorge leyó seis libros y ocho revistas el mes pasado. Leyó nueve libros más este mes. ¿Cuántos libros ha leído Jorge en total?

A medida que los niños aprendan a analizar problemas, también formularán sus propios problemas usando las destrezas que adquieran en cada lección. Los niños compartirán y resolverán estos problemas durante el festival de problemas al final de la unidad.

Si tiene alguna duda o comentario, por favor comuníquese conmigo.

Atentamente,
El maestro de su niño

Teen Problems with Various Unknowns

Going Further

Fill in the blanks. Then cut out each card. Write and draw the answer on the back.

newspaper

Ty delivers _____ newspapers every Saturday. He delivers _____ papers every Sunday. How many papers does Ty deliver in all?

book

Rachel read _____ pages in her book last week. This week she read _____ pages. How many pages did she read in all?

penny

Mari had _____ pennies. Then she got some more pennies on her birthday. Now she has _____ pennies. How many pennies did she get on her birthday?

strawberry

Miguel has _____ berries. _____ are strawberries. The rest are blueberries. How many berries are blueberries?

Story Problems to 100

Class Activity

Write 4 things that might be found in each drawer.

Drinks

⟶

1. Juice
2. Milk
3. Lemonade
4. Water

1.

Balls

⟶

1. _____
2. _____
3. _____
4. _____

2.

Toys

⟶

1. _____
2. _____
3. _____
4. _____

3.

Fruits

⟶

1. _____
2. _____
3. _____
4. _____

Class Activity

Name _____

Vocabulary
label

Fill each drawer with 4 things that belong together.
Then **label** the drawers.

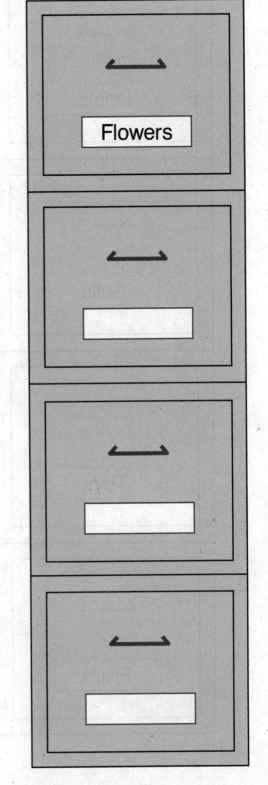

1. Tulip
2. Daisy
3. Rose
4. Violet

1.
1. _____
2. _____
3. _____
4. _____

2.
1. _____
2. _____
3. _____
4. _____

3.
1. _____
2. _____
3. _____
4. _____

Flowers

Introduction to Category Problems

Class Activity

Name _____

Vocabulary
label
unknown partner

1. **Label** the boxes. Draw a line to each thing that belongs inside. Decide how many are in each box.

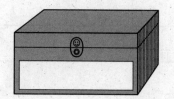 

←—Label

 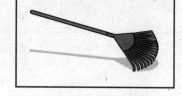 

_____ Shorts   _____ Rakes   _____ Dolls

  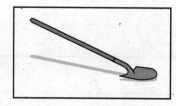

_____ Stuffed Animals   _____ Shirts   _____ Shovels

2. Write a story problem about one of the boxes you filled.

_____

- -

_____

_____

- -

_____

➡ 3. **On the Back** Write a story problem about another box. Use an **unknown partner**.

Name _____

Going Further

Vocabulary
label

Cut out the items below.

Glue the items that belong together in a

Venn Diagram on another piece of paper.

Label each group.

orange	football	book
computer	magazine	strawberry
soccer ball	calculator	tennis racket
dictionary	melon	pencil
baseball bat	newspaper	scissors
banana	ruler	television
telephone	notebook	crayons

Name _____

Going Further

1. Show different ways to get each number.

Ways to Get to 16

$\boxed{} + \boxed{} + \boxed{} = 16$

$\boxed{} + \boxed{} + \boxed{} = 16$

$16 = \boxed{} + \boxed{} + \boxed{} + \boxed{}$

$16 = \boxed{} + \boxed{} - \boxed{}$

Ways to Get to 13

$\boxed{} + \boxed{} + \boxed{} = 13$

$\boxed{} + \boxed{} + \boxed{} = 13$

$13 = \boxed{} + \boxed{} + \boxed{} + \boxed{}$

$13 = \boxed{} + \boxed{} - \boxed{}$

Ways to Get to 11

$\boxed{} + \boxed{} + \boxed{} = 11$

$\boxed{} + \boxed{} + \boxed{} = 11$

$11 = \boxed{} + \boxed{} + \boxed{} + \boxed{}$

$11 = \boxed{} + \boxed{} - \boxed{}$

Ways to Get to 18

$\boxed{} + \boxed{} + \boxed{} = 18$

$\boxed{} + \boxed{} + \boxed{} = 18$

$18 = \boxed{} + \boxed{} + \boxed{} + \boxed{}$

$18 = \boxed{} + \boxed{} - \boxed{}$

2. **On the Back** Write a story problem to go along with one of your equations. Solve it.

　　　　Multiple-Step Addition Problems **325**

Name _____

Multiple-Step Addition Problems

9-7

Extra Practice

Solve the story problems.

Show your work. Use drawings, numbers, or words.

1. Susan bought 7 muffins yesterday. Today she bought some more muffins. She bought 14 muffins in all. How many muffins did she buy today?

☐ _____
      label

2. A pet store has 8 parrots and some canaries. There are 17 birds altogether. How many of these birds are canaries?

☐ _____
      label

3. Mr. Ruben has 7 hammers and 5 saws. How many tools does he have?

☐ _____
      label

4. I have 5 red baseball caps, 4 black ones, and 6 blue ones. How many baseball caps do I have altogether?

☐ _____
      label

Extra Practice

Solve the story problems.

Show your work. Use drawings, numbers, or words.

5. Emma bought 3 bones for her puppy and 9 dog biscuits. The puppy ate 4 of the dog biscuits. How many dog treats are left?

[   ] _____
    label

6. Sarah ate 15 cherries. She ate 6 of them last night. Today she ate the rest. How many cherries did she eat today?

[   ] _____
    label

7. Our garden had 16 carrots yesterday. We ate 7 of them for dinner. Today there are 4 more carrots. How many carrots are there now?

[   ] _____
    label

8. Jeremy had 12 buttons on his coat. Now there are only 9. How many buttons did Jeremy lose?

[   ] _____
    label

Stories with Mixed Operations

Extra Practice

Vocabulary
equation

Solve the **equations**.

Match your total to a letter in the box.

Write the matching letter over the exercise
number at the bottom of the page.

50 is E	60 is R
84 is K	70 is O
49 is W	40 is A
98 is T	30 is G

1. $30 + 50 + 4$ = ☐

2. $60 - 10 - 10$ = ☐

3. $60 + 30 + 8$ = ☐

4. $80 + 10 - 40$ = ☐

5. $30 + 30 + 10$ = ☐

6. $70 + 10 - 20$ = ☐

7. $20 + 40 - 30$ = ☐

8. $20 + 20 + 9$ = ☐

9. $90 - 10 - 20$ = ☐

What will I say when you finish?

___ ___ ___ ___ ___ ___ ___ ___ ___ !
7.   9.   4.   2.   3.   8.   5.   6.   1.

10. **On the Back** Choose one of the equations on this page
and write a story problem for it.

Name

Multiple-Step Problems with Greater Numbers

Extra Practice

Cross out the **outsider**.

Write a name for each group on the line below.

1.
| apple |
| eye |
| grape |
| plum |
| peach |

2.
| baseball |
| soccer |
| tennis |
| nose |
| football |

3.
| ear |
| fish |
| dog |
| bird |
| cat |

4.
| shoe |
| pants |
| socks |
| shirt |
| mouth |

_____   _____   _____   _____

In box 5, write the outsiders from boxes 1–4.

5.

_____
_____
_____
_____

Name this group _____

Solve the story problem below.

Cross out the information you don't need.

6. My school has 14 black telephones,
   7 white telephones, and 15 computers.
   How many telephones are in my school? _____

➡ 7. **On the Back** Write your own story problem with
   extra information.

Find Essential Information

Class Activity

1. Measure the Fahrenheit and Celsius temperatures. Record the temperatures in the table.

Sample	Temperature	
Ice water	°F	°C
Cold tap water	°F	°C
Hot tap water	°F	°C

2. Write 2 statements that compare the temperatures you measured.

_____

_____

_____

3. Make a prediction. How long will take for the ice water temperature to change to 68°F?
My prediction:

_____

4. Check your prediction.
Record the temperature every
15 minutes in this table.

5. How long did it take?

_____

6. Compare your prediction to the actual time.

_____

_____

Time (min)	Temperature (°F)

Class Activity

Use the Number Path to skip count backward.

1. Start at 40. Skip count backward by 10s to 10.
   Write the numbers. ____ ____ ____ ____

2. How many times did you count backward by 10
   to go from 40 to 10? _____

3. Start at 70. Skip count backward by 10s to 10.
   Write the numbers.

   ____ ____ ____ ____ ____ ____

4. How many times did you count backward by 10
   to go from 70 to 10? _____

5. Predict how many times you will count
   backward by 10 from 60 to 10. _____

   Check your prediction.
   Write the numbers. Then count the times.

   ____ ____ ____ ____ ____

   Compare your prediction and your count.

6. Start at 50. Skip count backward by 5s to 20.
   Write the numbers.

   ____ ____ ____ ____ ____ ____ ____

7. Start at 50. Skip count backward by 10s to 20.
   Write the numbers. ____ ____ ____ ____

8. Why do you count more numbers to skip
   count by 5s than to skip count by 10s?

   _____

Name _____

Solve.

1. $9 - 3 + 4 =$ ⬜

2. $20 + 40 + 6 =$ ⬜

Solve the story problems.

Show your work. Use drawings, numbers, or words.

3. Yesterday, Dave picked 25 cherries. Today he picked some more. He picked 37 cherries in all. How many cherries did he pick today?

⬜ _____
  label

cherry

4. There were 23 deer. Some deer ran away. Now there are 16 deer left. How many deer ran away?

⬜ _____
  label

deer

Solve the story problems.

Show your work. Use drawings, numbers, or words.

---

5. The store sold 45 drills and 23 saws. How many tools did the store sell?

saw

```
┌──────┐  _____
│      │
└──────┘     label
```

---

6. Our yard has 29 trees. 8 are maple trees, and the rest are oak trees. How many are oak trees?

tree

```
┌──────┐  _____
│      │
└──────┘     label
```

---

7. Mark washed 10 blue shirts, 8 white socks, and 6 red shirts. How many shirts did he wash?

shirt

```
┌──────┐  _____
│      │
└──────┘     label
```

9

Unit Test

Name _____

Solve the story problems.

Show your work. Use drawings, numbers, or words.

---

8. The balloon man had 2 red balloons, 7 yellow balloons, and 3 orange balloons. How many balloons did he have in all?

balloon

◻ _____
　　　label

---

9. There were 9 people on the bus. Then 6 people got off and 2 people got on. How many people are on the bus now?

bus

◻ _____
　　　label

10. Extended Response Write a story problem. Solve it.

Going Further

Trace around your hands and your feet.
Cut out your paper hands and feet.
Use them to measure objects in the room.

1. Compare your hand and foot. Which is longer? _____

2. Find two things longer than your hand. _____

_____

3. Find two things about the same length as your foot. _____

_____

4. Take 3 giant steps. About how many of your hand lengths are

   your 3 giant steps? _____

5. About how many of your foot lengths are your

   3 giant steps? _____

Find two things to measure. Write the name of each
thing and how many of your hands or feet long it is.

6. I measured _____.

   It is about _____ long.

7. I measured _____.

   It is about _____ long.

8. **On the Back** Draw a picture of your pencil. Then use a
   paper clip to measure it. About how many paper clips long
   is your pencil?

Measurement: Nonstandard Units and Rounding **341**

Measurement: Nonstandard Units and Rounding

Family Letter

Dear Family:

Your child has begun a math unit that focuses on measurement. Measurement is an important mathematical skill, and it is one that is easily applied to daily life.

The children will start measuring with nonstandard units such as colored strips of paper, toothpicks, hands, and feet. Using these items to measure helps children understand the concepts of measurement and units.

The class will move quickly from using nonstandard units to measuring with both inch and centimeter rulers. Children are encouraged to estimate lengths before they measure them.

Another concept introduced in this unit is rounding. The children practice rounding to the nearest unit or number.

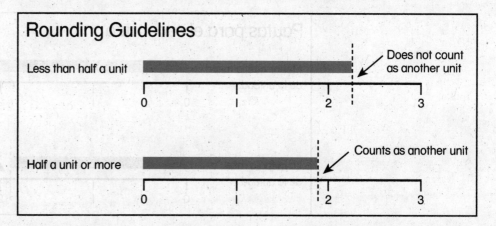

You can help your child practice estimating, measuring, and rounding at home. If you have any questions, please contact me.

Sincerely,
Your child's teacher

Carta a la familia

Estimada familia:

Su niño ha empezado una unidad que trata de la medición. La medición es una destreza matemática importante y se aplica fácilmente en la vida diaria.

Los niños empezarán a medir con unidades de medida no usuales, como tiras de papel, palillos de dientes, manos y pies. Estos objetos ayudan a los niños a comprender el concepto de medición y de las unidades.

La clase pasará rápidamente de usar unidades no usuales a medir con reglas de pulgadas y centímetros. Se anima a los niños a estimar longitudes antes de medirlas.

Otro concepto que se presenta en esta unidad es el redondeo. Los niños practican el redondeo a la unidad o número más cercano.

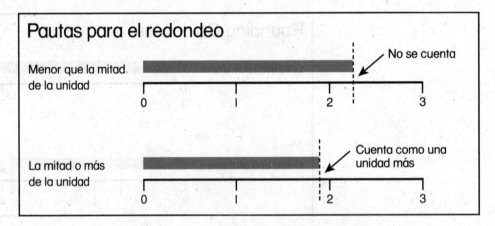

Usted puede ayudar a su niño a practicar la estimación, la medición y el redondeo en casa. Si tiene alguna duda, por favor comuníquese conmigo.

Atentamente,
El maestro de su niño

Measurement: Nonstandard Units and Rounding

Name _____

Vocabulary
measure
inch (in.)
estimate

1. **Measure** each pencil. Round to the nearest **inch**.

about ☐ inches

about ☐ inches

about ☐ inches

2. **Estimate** how many inches.
Then measure and write the length.

Estimate: about ☐ inches   Measure: ☐ inches

Estimate: about ☐ inches   Measure: ☐ inches

Estimate: about ☐ inches   Measure: ☐ inches

Estimate each line **length**.

Then measure each line with an inch ruler.

1.

Estimate

Measure

☐ in. ☐ in.

2.

Estimate

Measure

☐ in. ☐ in.

3.

Estimate

Measure

☐ in. ☐ in.

4.

Estimate

Measure

☐ in. ☐ in.

5.

Estimate

Measure

☐ in. ☐ in.

6.

Estimate

Measure

☐ in. ☐ in.

Use an Inch Ruler

Class Activity

Measure each line or shape.

Round to the nearest **inch**.

1.

c.

a. about ☐ in.

b. about ☐ in.

b.

c. about ☐ in.

a.

2.

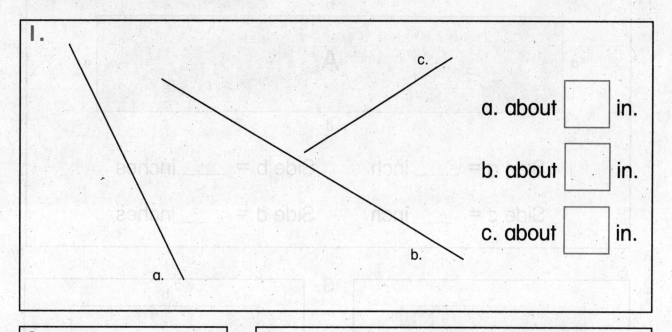

a.　　　b.

c.

a. about ☐ in.

b. about ☐ in.

c. about ☐ in.

3.

b.

a.　　　c.

d.

a. about ☐ in.　　b. about ☐ in.

c. about ☐ in.　　d. about ☐ in.

Class Activity

Name _____

Measure the sides of each box with an inch ruler.

1.

b

a   **A**   c

d

Side a = _____ inch   Side b = _____ inches

Side c = _____ inch   Side d = _____ inches

2.

b

a   **B**   c

d

Side a = _____ inch

Side b = _____ inches

Side c = _____ inch

Side d = _____ inches

3.

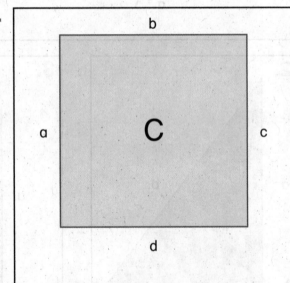

b

a   **C**   c

d

Side a = _____ inches

Side b = _____ inches

Side c = _____ inches

Side d = _____ inches

4. Which shape is a square?
Ring the letter below.

A   B   C

Measure Shapes in Inches

Class Activity

Vocabulary
measure
centimeter (cm)
estimate

Measure each piece of yarn to the nearest **centimeter**.

1. about ☐ cm

2. about ☐ cm

3. about ☐ cm

4. about ☐ cm

Estimate how many centimeters.
Then measure and write the length.

5.

Estimate: about ☐ cm   Measure: ☐ cm

6.

Estimate: about ☐ cm   Measure: ☐ cm

7.

Estimate: about ☐ cm   Measure: ☐ cm

Class Activity

Object	Estimate	Centimeters
1		
2		
3		
4		
5		
6		
7		
8		
9		

Use a Centimeter Ruler

Vocabulary
measure
centimeter (cm)

Measure the sides of the shapes. Write the numbers of **centimeters** next to the sides. Then color the shapes.

Color the triangles △ yellow.

Color the rectangles ▭ red.

Color the trapezoids ▱ orange.

Color the squares ▪ blue.

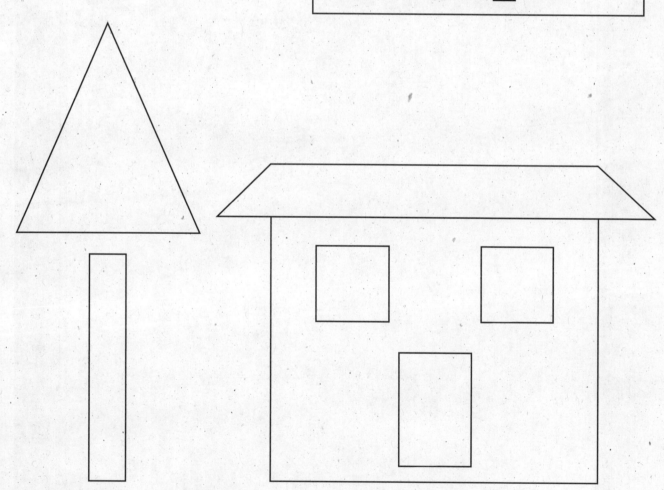

⊃**On the Back** Draw a picture with 3 different shapes.

Use a Centimeter Ruler

Measure the **length** and **width** in centimeters of each **rectangle** below.

Vocabulary
length
width
rectangle

1.

A

length
☐ cm

width
☐ cm

2.

B

length
☐ cm

width
☐ cm

3.

C

length
☐ cm

width
☐ cm

4.

D

length
☐ cm

width
☐ cm

Name _____

Class Activity

Vocabulary
length
width

1. Write the **length** and **width** of each rectangle you measured.
   Is it a square? Write yes or no in the last space.

Rectangle	Length	Width	Square?
A			
B			
C			
D			

2. Draw your own square below.
   Write its measurements.

length [ ] cm   width [ ] cm

Measure Shapes in Centimeters

Going Further

Vocabulary
centimeter (cm)

Measure each side with a **centimeter** ruler.
Write an equation to find the distance around
each shape.

1.

___ + ___ + ___ + ___ = ☐
cm

2.

___ + ___ + ___ = ☐
cm

3.

___ + ___ + ___ + ___ = ☐
cm

4.

___ + ___ + ___ + ___ = ☐
cm

➡ 5. **On the Back** Draw a shape. Measure each side
to the nearest centimeter. Use the measures to
find the distance around the shape.

Measure Shapes in Centimeters

Vocabulary
inch (in.)
centimeter (cm)

Measure objects in your classroom.
Measure in both **inches** and **centimeters**.
Round the numbers.

Object	Centimeters	Inches
Book		
Pencil		
Eraser		

Going Further

Vocabulary
measure
unit

1. **Measure** your object with 3 different **units**. Write the number and unit.

Object _____

Measure: about [ ] _____
unit

Measure: about [ ] _____
unit

Measure: about [ ] _____
unit

2. Draw a picture of your object.

Comparative Measurements: Centimeters and Inches

Vocabulary

pound

Use a balance scale and a 1-**pound** weight.

Weigh each object. Put an X in the matching box.

Object	Less than 1 pound	About 1 pound	More than 1 pound

Class Activity

Use a 1-**liter** bottle and water. Measure how much each object holds. Put an X in the matching box. Find more objects to measure.

Object	Holds less than 1 liter	Holds about 1 liter	Holds more than 1 liter
Cup			
Pitcher			
Bucket			

Weight and Capacity

Class Activity

Name

Vocabulary

estimate

Ring one group of ten. **Estimate** about how many in all. Count to check.

1.

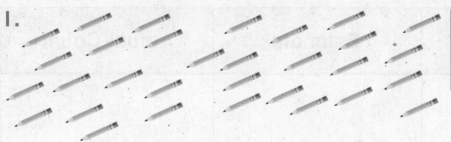

Estimate	Actual Count

2.

Estimate	Actual Count

3.

Estimate	Actual Count

4.

Estimate	Actual Count

Estimate Quantities and Sums **361**

Class Activity

Find groups of objects in your classroom.
Make an estimate. Count to check.

Object	Estimate	Actual Count

Name _____

Vocabulary
estimate
measure

Estimate which object weighs more. Write or draw your estimate.

Use a balance scale to **measure**. Record or draw your measurement.

Which Weighs More?

Objects	Estimate	Measure
Book Box of crayons		
Scissors Tape dispenser		
Pencil Paper clip		

Vocabulary
estimate
holds more
measure

Estimate which **holds more**. Write or draw your estimate.

Measure. Fill each container with cups of sand or water.

Record or draw the number of cups.

Which Holds More?

Containers	Estimate	Measure
Mug Pitcher		
Milk carton Bowl		
Teacup Bucket		

Estimate Weight and Capacity

Name _____

Estimate how many inches.
Then measure and write the length.

1.

Estimate: about ☐ inches   Measure: ☐ inches

2.

Estimate: about ☐ inches   Measure: ☐ inches

3.

Estimate: about ☐ inches   Measure: ☐ inches

4.

Estimate: about ☐ inches   Measure: ☐ inches

5.

Estimate: about ☐ inches   Measure: ☐ inches

Measure the shape. Round to the nearest inch.

6.

Side a is about _____ in.

Side b is about _____ in.

Side c is about _____ in.

Side d is about _____ in.

Unit Test

Name

Use an inch ruler.

Measure the length and width of each rectangle.

7.

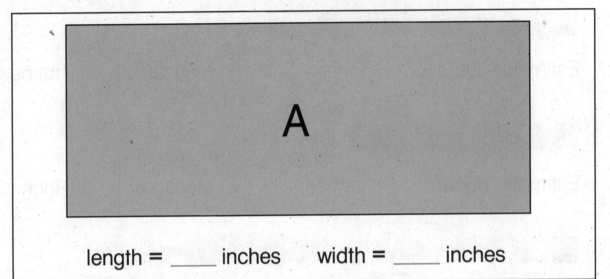

length = _____ inches   width = _____ inches

8.

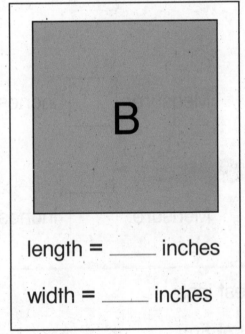

length = _____ inches

width = _____ inches

9.

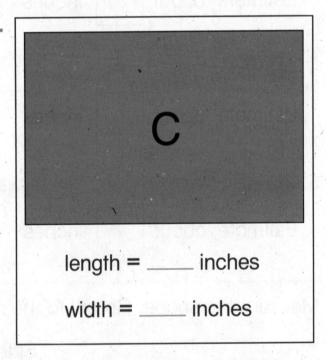

length = _____ inches

width = _____ inches

10. Which shape is a square? Look at the shapes A, B, and C above. Ring the letter below.

A   B   C

Test

Estimate how many centimeters.

Then measure and write the length.

11.

Estimate: about [ ] cm   Measure: [ ] cm

12.

Estimate: about [ ] cm   Measure: [ ] cm

13.

Estimate: about [ ] cm   Measure: [ ] cm

14.

Estimate: about [ ] cm   Measure: [ ] cm

15.

Estimate: about [ ] cm   Measure: [ ] cm

Measure each side. Round to the nearest centimeter.

16.

Side a is about ____ cm.

Side b is about ____ cm.

Side c is about ____ cm.

Side d is about ____ cm.

Use a centimeter ruler.

Measure the length and width of each rectangle.

17.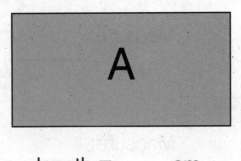

length = _____ cm

width = _____ cm

18.

length = _____ cm

width = _____ cm

19. Which shape is a square? Look at the shapes A and B above. Ring the letter below.

A   B

20. **Extended Response** How can you measure to find a square? Explain.

_____

- -

_____

- -

_____

- -

_____

Class Activity

Use the **number line**.

Write the missing numbers.

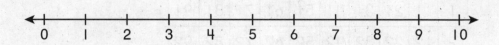

1. 1, ____, ____, 4, ____, ____, ____, 8

2. 3, 4, ____, ____, ____, ____, ____, 10

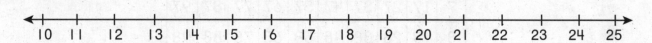

3. 10, 11, ____, 13, 14, ____, 16

4. 19, ____, 21, ____, ____, ____

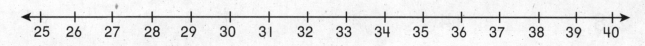

5. 26, ____, 28, ____, ____

6. ____, ____, ____, ____, 37

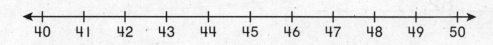

7. 46, ____, ____, ____, 50

8. ____, 43, ____, ____, ____

Class Activity

Name _____

Vocabulary

skip count

Skip count by 2s.

Write the missing numbers.

1	11	21	31	41	51	61	71	81	91
2	12	22	32	42	52	62	72	82	92
3	13	23	33	43	53	63	73	83	93
4	14	24	34	44	54	64	74	84	94
5	15	25	35	45	55	65	75	85	95
6	16	26	36	46	56	66	76	86	96
7	17	27	37	47	57	67	77	87	97
8	18	28	38	48	58	68	78	88	98
9	19	29	39	49	59	69	79	89	99
10	20	30	40	50	60	70	80	90	100

1. 2, _____, _____, 8

2. 8, _____, _____, 14

3. 22, _____, _____, 28

4. 54, 56, _____, _____, 62

5. 76, _____, _____, 82, _____, _____

6. 16, _____, _____, _____, _____, 26

7. 48, _____, _____, 54, 56, _____, _____

8. 82, 84, _____, _____, 90, _____, _____

Identify and Represent Numbers

Class Activity

Name _____

Use the number line to **add**.

Draw arrows. Solve.

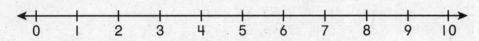

1. $5 + 2 =$ _____

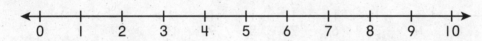

2. $3 + 7 =$ _____

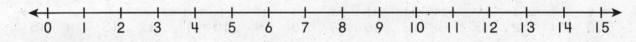

3. $8 + 6 =$ _____

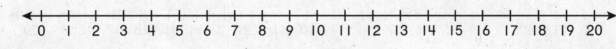

4. _____ $= 8 + 9$

Class Activity

Name _____

Use the number line to **subtract**.

Draw arrows. Solve.

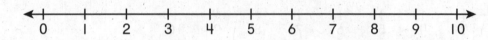

1. 10 – 3 = _____

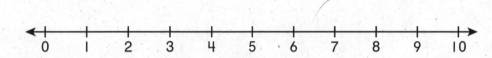

2. 8 – 4 = _____

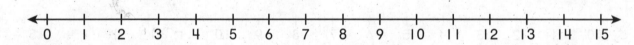

3. 14 – 6 = _____

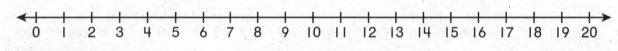

4. _____ = 18 – 9

Class Activity

Name

Read and discuss the example below.

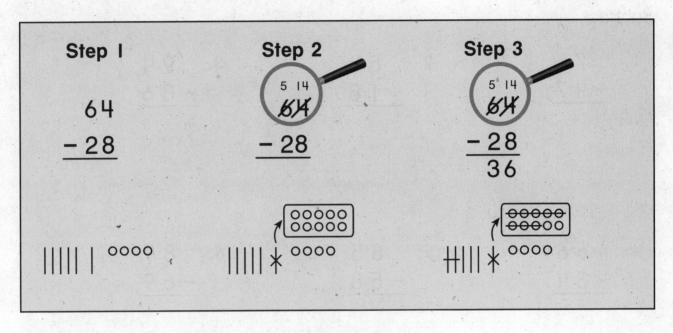

Subtract. Use the **Ungroup First Method**.

Make a proof drawing to show your work.

1. 52
   − 29

2. 65
   − 36

3. 83
   − 39

Class Activity

Subtract.

1.   75
     −47
	2. 54
	     −18
		3. 94
		     −36

4.   66
     −34
	5. 85
	     −58
		6. 89
		     −69

7.   82
     −59
	8. 97
	     −78
		9. 65
		     −28

10.   78
     −19
	11. 53
	     −26
		12. 91
		     −46

Class Activity

Name _____

Vocabulary

tally chart
line plot

Five friends wanted to see what spelling score they made most often.

Spelling Scores				
Elizabeth	10	8	8	9
Wayne	8	9	6	8
Benjamin	9	7	9	10
Sophia	7	6	8	8
Alyce	9	7	9	8

They made a **tally chart** of the scores.

Score	Tally
10	II
9	IIII I
8	IIII II
7	III
6	II

Then they made a **line plot**. In a line plot, each piece of data is shown with an x.

Spelling Scores

```
                  X
                  X        X
                  X        X
                  X        X
          X       X        X
   X      X       X        X       X
   X      X       X        X       X
 ───────────────────────────────────
   6      7       8        9       10
```

Why is it easy to see the score that was made most often in the line plot?

Name _____

Class Activity

1. Take turns. Roll the number cube 20 times in all.
   Record the number rolled each time on the **tally chart**.

Number Rolled

Number	Tally
1	
2	
3	
4	
5	
6	

2. Make a **line plot**.
   Use the data from your tally chart.

Number Rolled

```
  |——————————————————————————————————
  1     2     3     4     5     6
```

Tally Charts and Line Plots

Class Activity

Name _____

Vocabulary

multiplication

I have 5 pairs of socks. How many socks do I have all together?

1 2   3 4   5 6   7 8   9 10

             5 × 2 = __10__

2 + 2 + 2 + 2 + 2 = __10__

Complete the addition and **multiplication** equation for each story. Make a math drawing to help you solve the problem.

_____

1. I have 3 dogs. Each dog has 4 bones. How many bones are there?

    4 + 4 + 4 = _____

    3 × 4 = _____

    _____
    label

_____

2. I have 5 vases. There are 2 flowers in each vase. How many flowers are there?

    2 + 2 + 2 + 2 + 2 = _____

    5 × 2 = _____

    _____
    label

_____

3. I eat 4 vegetables every day. How many vegetables do I eat in 5 days?

    4 + 4 + 4 + 4 + 4 = _____

    5 × 4 = _____

    _____
    label

Class Activity

Name _____

Vocabulary

array

Look at each **array**. Write the numbers.

1. ⊙⊙⊙⊙ / ⊙⊙⊙⊙

_____ × _____ or

_____ × _____

2. ⊙⊙⊙⊙⊙ / ⊙⊙⊙⊙⊙ / ⊙⊙⊙⊙⊙

_____ × _____ or

_____ × _____

3.

_____ × _____ or

_____ × _____

4.

_____ × _____

5. Draw your own array. Label your array 2 ways.

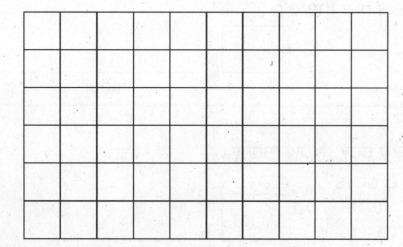

_____ × _____

_____ × _____

Represent Multiplication

Glossary

Glossary (Continued)

5-group

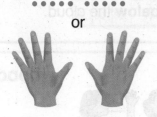
← 5-group

10-group

or

10-stick

||| ○○

There are 3 **10-sticks** in 32.

A

above

The sun is **above** the cloud.

add

●●● ●●

3 + 2 = 5

addend

5 + 4 = 9
↑ ↑
addends

addition story problem

There are 5 ducks.
Then 3 more come.
How many ducks are there now?

after

98, 99

99 is **after** 98.

apart

Amy pulls her hands **apart**.

Glossary (Continued)

E

equal partners

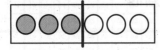

equal shares

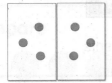

equal shares of 6

equal to (=)

4 + 4 = 8

4 plus 4 is **equal to** 8.

equation

Examples:

4 + 3 = 7   7 = 4 + 3

9 − 5 = 4   4 = 9 − 5

estimate

You can **estimate** the length of an object.

I estimate the paper clip is about 1 inch long.

You can estimate the number of objects in a set.

about 10

even number

A number is even if you can make groups of 2 and have none left over.

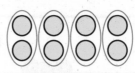

8 is an **even number**.

F

fewer

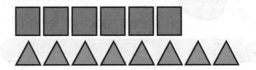

There are **fewer** ▊ than ▲.

fewest

Eggs Laid This Month

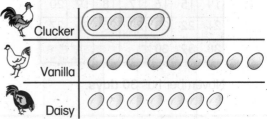

Clucker laid the **fewest** eggs.

flip

You can **flip** a figure over a horizontal line.

You can **flip** a figure over a vertical line.

forward

Sahil is walking **forward**.

fraction

4 equal parts $\frac{1}{4}$ is 1 out of 4 equal parts.

The **fraction** of the square that is shaded is $\frac{1}{4}$.

G

greater than

1, 2, 3, 4, 5, 6, 7

7 is **greater than** 3.

grid

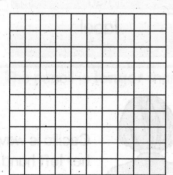

H

half-hour

minute hand

A **half-hour** is 30 minutes.

hour

hour hand

An **hour** is 60 minutes.

hundred

1	11	21	31	41	51	61	71	81	91
2	12	22	32	42	52	62	72	82	92
3	13	23	33	43	53	63	73	83	93
4	14	24	34	44	54	64	74	84	94
5	15	25	35	45	55	65	75	85	95
6	16	26	36	46	56	66	76	86	96
7	17	27	37	47	57	67	77	87	97
8	18	28	38	48	58	68	78	88	98
9	19	29	39	49	59	69	79	89	99
10	20	30	40	50	60	70	80	90	100

or

Glossary (Continued)

month

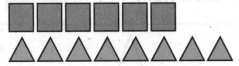

		June				
Sun	Mon	Tues	Wed	Thurs	Fri	Sat
				1	2	3
4	5	6	7	8	9	10
11	12	13	14	15	16	17
18	19	20	21	22	23	24
25	26	27	28	29	30	

June is the sixth **month**.

There are twelve months in a year.

more

There are **more** △ than ■.

most

Eggs Laid This Month

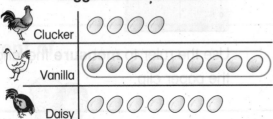

Vanilla laid the **most** eggs.

N

next to

Sara is **next to** Alex.

Sara   Alex

nickel

5¢ or 5 cents

not equal to (≠)

6 ≠ 8

6 is **not equal to** 8.

number sentence

4 + 3 = 7
or
7 = 4 + 3

9 − 5 = 4
or
4 = 9 − 5

O

odd number

A number is odd if you can make groups of 2 and have one left over.

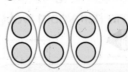

7 is an **odd number**.

one fourth

1 whole

$\frac{1}{4}$

one half

I whole

$\frac{1}{2}$

one third

I whole

$\frac{1}{3}$

ones

ones

56 has 6 **ones**.

ordinal numbers

first, second, third, fourth, fifth
sixth, seventh, eighth, ninth, tenth

Ordinal numbers tell the position of things in order.

out, outside

Evan's hand is **outside** the box.

oval

P

pair

a **pair** of counters

a **pair** of shoes

partner

5 = 2 + 3

2 and 3 are **partners** of 5.
2 and 3 are 5-**partners**.

partner house

```
        9
     5 + 4
     6 + 3
     3 + 6
     4 + 5
     7 + 2
     8 + 1
     2 + 7
     1 + 8
```

Glossary (Continued)

partner train

4-train

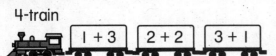

pattern

2, 4, 6, 8, 10, 12

These are **patterns**.

penny

1¢ or 1 cent

pentagons

A **pentagon** has 5 sides.

picture graph

| Flowers | 🌸🌸🌸🌸🌸🌸 |
| Vases | 🏺🏺🏺🏺🏺🏺🏺🏺 |

plus

3 + 2 = 5

$$\begin{array}{r} 3 \\ + 2 \\ \hline 5 \end{array}$$

3 **plus** 2 equals 5.

quarter

25¢ or 25 cents

rectangles

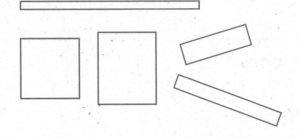

rectangular prism

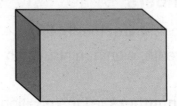

related equations

5 + 3 = 8
50 + 30 = 80

repeating pattern

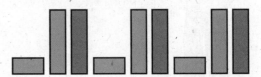

right

Cecilia is waving her **right** hand.

row

1	11	21	31	41	51	61	71	81	91
2	12	22	32	42	52	62	72	82	92
3	13	23	33	43	53	63	73	83	93
4	14	24	34	44	54	64	74	84	94
5	15	25	35	45	55	65	75	85	95
6	16	26	36	46	56	66	76	86	96
7	17	27	37	47	57	67	77	87	97
8	18	28	38	48	58	68	78	88	98
9	19	29	39	49	59	69	79	89	99
10	20	30	40	50	60	70	80	90	100

ruler

A **ruler** is used to measure length.

S

shapes

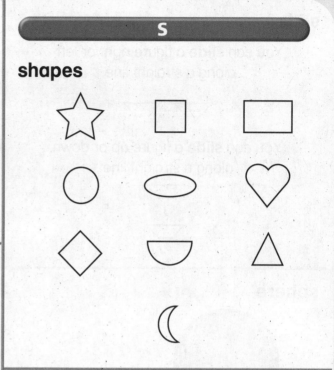

shorter

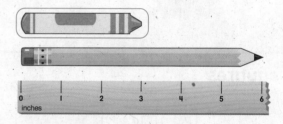

The crayon is **shorter** than the pencil.

side

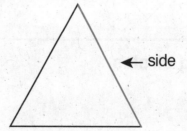

← side

Glossary (Continued)

slide

You can **slide** a figure right or left along a straight line.

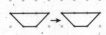

You can **slide** a figure up or down along a straight line.

sphere

squares

sticks and circles

I   ○

II | ○

21 || ○

31 ||| ○

subtract

8 − 3 = 5

○○○○○ ○○○

subtraction story problem

8 flies are on a log.
6 are eaten by a frog.
How many flies are left?

sum

4 + 3 = 7   4
                  + 3
         sum →   7

sum →

switch the partners

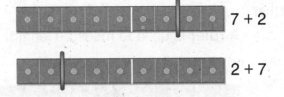

7 + 2

2 + 7

symmetry

A shape has **symmetry** if it can be folded along a line so that the two halves match exactly.

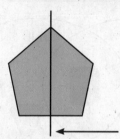

← line of symmetry

T

table

Instruments	Number
Horns	4
Violins	5
Drums	3
Guitars	5

teen number

11 12 13 14 15 16 17 18 19
teen numbers

teen total

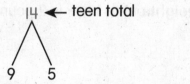

14 ← teen total

9   5

tens

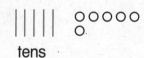

tens

56 has 5 **tens**.

together

Put your hands **together**.

total

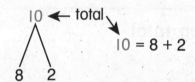

4 + 3 = 7

4
+ 3
total → 7

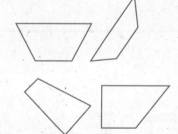

10 ← total

10 = 8 + 2

8   2

trapezoids

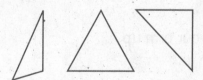

triangles

Glossary (Continued)

turn

You can **turn** a shape around a point.

unknown partner

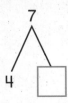

7

4 ☐

4 + ☐ = 7

unknown total

☐

5 3

5 + 3 = ☐

up

Put your arm **up**.

Venn diagram

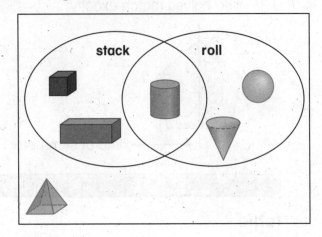

stack   roll

vertical form

$$\begin{array}{r} 6 \\ + 3 \\ \hline 9 \end{array}$$

weight

2 lb

The **weight** of this book is 2 pounds.

width

length

width

or

width

length

word name

12

twelve ← word name

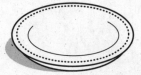

Z

zero

There are **zero** apples on the plate.

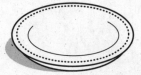